Case Studies in
Culture and Communication

Case Studies in Culture and Communication

A Group Perspective

James A. Schnell

LEXINGTON BOOKS
Lanham • Boulder • New York • Oxford

LEXINGTON BOOKS

Published in the United States of America
by Lexington Books
An imprint of The Rowman & Littlefield Publishing Group, Inc.
4501 Forbes Boulevard, Suite 200, Lanham, Maryland 20706

PO Box 317
Oxford
OX2 9RU, UK

British Library Cataloguing in Publication Information Available

Library of Congress Cataloging-in-Publication Data

Schnell, James A., 1955–
    Case studies in culture and communication : a group perspective / James A. Schnell.
        p. cm.
    Includes bibliographical references and index.
    ISBN 0-7391-0583-3 (cloth)
    1. Communication—Social aspects. 2. Intercultural communication. I. Title.

    HM561.S36 2003
    302.2—dc21   2003005575

Printed in the United States of America

⊖™ The paper used in this publication meets the minimum requirements of American
National Standard for Information Sciences—Permanence of Paper for Printed Library
Materials, ANSI/NISO Z39.48–1992.

This book is dedicated to my wife, our son,
and our life together.

Contents

Introduction

This book presents case study analyses of phenomena evolving from the relationship between culture and communication. A group perspective is employed. Three areas of analyses are addressed: case studies in American culture, case studies in cross-cultural contexts, and case studies in applied settings. These case studies are drawn from my research stressing culture and communication.

Most of my study has dealt with the relationship between culture and communication and a significant portion of that research has focused on cross-cultural issues. My international travel has significantly affected my academic development. Such travel has included over forty-seven trips outside of the United States, to all the continents, except Antarctica. This travel has been as a civilian and as a member of the U.S. military.

Section One

CASE STUDIES IN
AMERICAN CULTURE

Chapter One

Ross Perot's Expression of Sensitivity and Insensitivity with Diversity Issues during the 1992 Presidential Campaign

In the spring of 1992, Texas businessman Ross Perot rose from relative obscurity to become a major contender for the U.S. presidency. Six months after indicating an interest in being president while appearing on *Larry King Live*, he received 19 percent of the popular vote in the 1992 presidential campaign. Perot's primary strength was his emphasis on the U.S. economy and his intention to promote job growth. A weakness for Perot was the public perception that he was insensitive to diversity issues in America. The surest way to study this insensitivity is to analyze Perot's public presentations.

The hypothesis for this chapter is that Perot's presentations will contain statements conveying insensitivity with diversity issues. The formulation of this hypothesis is based primarily on newspaper reports of Perot's June 11, 1992, speech to the NAACP convention. The *Washington Post* reported "Perot drew a cool reception from the group when he referred to Blacks as 'you people' and 'your people'" (*Washington Post*, July 12, 1992). The *Chicago Tribune* referred to Perot's use of "you people" and "your people" as "a gaffe in his speech that offended some in the audience as racially insensitive" (*Chicago Tribune*, July 12, 1992).

"The expressions are something you do not use with African Americans. 'Never,' said Lacy Steele . . . a member of the NAACP's national board from Washington, D.C. . . . Many African Americans find the words offensive when coming from a White speaker" (*Chicago Tribune*, July 12, 1992). Perot's use of "you people" and "your people," as reported by the *Washington Post*, is included in the statement "I don't have to tell you who gets hurt when this sort of thing (economic crunch) happens—you people do. Your people do" (*Washing-

ton Post, 1992). This speech is significant in that Perot withdrew from the presidential race within five days of his NAACP speech.

The method for this inquiry is analysis of videotapes of Perot's appearances. The videotapes, recorded by C-SPAN, were obtained from the Public Affairs Video Archives (located at Purdue University). The Archives provided an index listing all of Perot's presentations delivered during the presidential campaign period (January-November 1992) that were covered by C-SPAN. A total of fifty-five presentations are available on videotape. Fourteen of these videotapes, representative of Perot's presentations in content, context, and formats, were selected for analysis. The content and context of his speeches were studied to see if there was evidence to support the claim made by Perot critics that Perot was insensitive toward diversity issues.

The following is a list of the selected videotapes. Title, date, format, and length are listed for each presentation.

1. Life and Career of Ross Perot (3/18/92)
   American Profile Interview (:13)
2. Perot Candidacy: American Newspaper Publishers Association (5/5/92)
   Speech (:34)
3. University of Oklahoma Commencement Address (5/9/92)
   Speech (:21)
4. Perot Campaign Speech: NAACP Annual Convention (7/11/92)
   Speech (:35)
5. Perot Withdrawal (7/16/92)
   News Conference (:20)
6. Perot Campaign Commercial (10/6/92)
   Broadcast (:29)
7. Presidential Candidates Debate (10/11/92)
   Debate (1:36)
8. Presidential Candidates Debate (10/15/92)
   Debate (1:32)
9. Perot Campaign Commercial (10/15/92)
   Broadcast (:30)
10. Presidential Candidates Debate (10/19/92)
    Debate (1:38)
11. Perot Campaign Commercial (10/20/92)
    Speech (:31)
12. Perot Campaign Commercial (10/26/92)
    Broadcast (:31)
13. Perot Campaign Commercial (10/28/92)
    Political Event (:28)
14. Perot Campaign Commercial (10/30/92)
    Broadcast (:29)

There is no widely accepted paradigm for analyzing a speaker's sensitivity with diversity issues so this inquiry poses unique challenges. What connotes sensitivity? What connotes insensitivity? Use of C-SPAN tapes to study the aforementioned subject is particularly relevant in that the C-SPAN index helps define the sample to be studied and the tapes provide literal verbal meanings, indirect nonverbal meanings, and context for speeches. Transcripts provide literal statements but the tapes frame the literal statements. Perot was criticized after his July 11, 1992, speech to the NAACP convention, according to the Public Affairs Video Archives index abstract for his "apparent paternalistic nature" toward minorities. Analysis of this type of criticism rests on what is said and, equally important, on how it is said.

Data relevant to the research question of this inquiry, regarding Perot's sensitivity/insensitivity toward minority issues, was studied by viewing all the aforementioned videotapes. This data includes ten hours and thirty-seven minutes of videotape. The data clearly disproves the hypothesis of this study (that Perot's presentations would contain statements conveying insensitivity with diversity issues). Perot's statements consistently convey sensitivity with diversity issues.

The videotapes were observed for any references to diversity in America. All of Perot's references to diversity, whether they be direct statements or indirect responses to questions, reflected sensitivity with diversity issues. Each of these references (to diversity) will be described to show the consistency in Perot's perspective.

On March 18, 1992, C-SPAN broadcast an American Profile Interview entitled "Life and Career of Ross Perot" (Perot, 3/18/92). During the interview, Perot mentioned how his father's support of African Americans influenced his own perspective and that one of his first philanthropic gifts was to an experimental school for disadvantaged (mainly minority) youth. Interviewer Brian Lamb asked what his response would be if the public, via an electronic town hall, wanted racial segregation rather than integration. Perot responded: "It's not constitutional. . . . We're not gonna turn the clock back. Segregating would hurt the economy."

Perot spoke to the American Newspaper Publishers Association on May 5, 1992. During this speech he stated, "If you hate other people I don't want your vote. . . . If you don't mind living in a society where one out of eight women are raped I don't want your vote" (Perot, 5/5/92).

Perot's speech to the NAACP convention on July 11, 1992, contained numerous statements related to diversity in America. "You have made tremendous progress but there's more to be done. . . . You people do, your people do [regarding who is most affected during an economic crunch]. . . . Our diversity is our strength, not a weakness . . . we ought to love one another, at least get along. . . . Divided teams lose, united teams win. . . . If you hate people I don't want your vote. . . . Drugs are devastating you and your people. . . . Our country will not be great until we are all united and equal. . . . I cannot be free until we are all free" (Perot, 7/11/92). He also described how his mother and father raised him to be sensitive to the plight of Blacks and the disadvantaged (Perot, 7/11/92).

During the presidential candidates debate on October 11, 1992, Perot restated many of his views from his NAACP convention speech. Perot stated, "We shouldn't appeal to the differences between us. . . . We should love one another. . . . Our diversity is our strength, we've turned it into a weakness. . . . Divided teams lose, united teams win. . . . If you hate people I don't want your vote" (Perot, 10/11/92).

Perot was asked during the October 15, 1992, presidential candidates debate when either political party will have a Black or woman on its ticket. He responded that Colin Powell could be on either party's ticket in four years (Perot, 10/15/92).

A reporter asked Perot, "Why aren't women and ethnic minorities better represented in upper levels of government?" during the October 19, 1992, presidential candidates debate. Perot answered the inquiry acknowledging that women have done very well in the computer industry (Perot's business background) and women are part of his team (Perot 10/19/92).

In a Perot campaign commercial broadcast October 20, 1992, he again spoke of his philanthropic efforts with the Dunbar School in 1968. The Dunbar School was a school for disadvantaged youth (including Blacks and Hispanics) to help them prepare for the first grade (Perot, 10/20/92).

The only speech containing comments perceived offensive is the 7/11/92 speech to the NAACP convention. In this speech Perot's referral to the Black audience as "you people" and "your people" was perceived by some to be racially insensitive. However, the NAACP is a self-defined organization comprised of African Americans. To refer to such a group as a distinctive entity, which the organization does with its name and objective, does not substantiate Perot as insensitive to diversity issues. The aforementioned Perot quotes clearly establish his sensitivity with American diversity.

Perot's candidacy sparked considerable debate. Scholars will no doubt be defining Perot's future in reference to his past. Findings from this type of study, contrasting the words of a person against his or her public image, helps to reinforce accurate observations and correct misconceptions.

Notes

Chicago Tribune. July 12, 1992, 6.

Jamieson, Kathleen Hall. *Eloquence in an Electronic Age: The Transformation of Political Speechmaking.* New York: Oxford University Press, 1988.

Kendall, Kathleen. "Public Speaking in the Presidential Primaries: Through Media Eyes." Paper presented at the Off the (Video) Record research conference, sponsored by the Public Affairs Video Archives (Purdue University, 1992).

Lanzetta, John T.; Sullivan, Denis G.; Masters, Roger D.; and McHugo, Gregory J. "Viewers' Emotional and Cognitive Responses to Televised Images of Political

Leaders," in Sidney Kraus and Richard Perloff, eds., *Mass Media and Political Thought.* Beverly Hills, CA: Sage, 1985.

Masters, Roger D. "Using Television to Study Presidential Politics." Paper presented at the Off the (Video) Record research conference, sponsored by the Public Affairs Video Archives (Purdue University, 1992).

McHugo, Gregory J., Lanzetta, John T., Sullivan, Denis G., Masters, Roger D., and Englis, Basil. "Emotional Reactions to Expressive Displays of a Political Leader," *Journal of Personality and Social Psychology*, 49 (1985), 1512-29.

Muir, Jannette K. *C-SPAN in the Communication Classroom: Theory and Application.* Annandale, VA: Speech Communication Association, 1992.

Perot, Ross. (3/18/92). "Life and Career of Ross Perot," C-SPAN American Profile Interview, Purdue University: Public Affairs Video Archives, 1992.

Perot, Ross. (5/5/92). "Perot Candidacy: American Newspaper Publishers Association," C-SPAN recorded Speech, Purdue University: Public Affairs Video Archives, 1992.

Perot, Ross. (7/11/92). "Perot Campaign Speech: NAACP Annual Convention," C-SPAN recorded Speech, Purdue University: Public Affairs Video Archives, 1992.

Perot, Ross. (10/11/92). "Presidential Candidates Debate," C-SPAN recorded Debate, Purdue University: Public Affairs Video Archives, 1992.

Perot, Ross. (10/15/92). "Presidential Candidates Debate," C-SPAN recorded Debate, Purdue University: Public Affairs Video Archives, 1992.

Perot, Ross. (10/19/92). "Presidential Candidates Debate," C-SPAN recorded Debate, Purdue University: Public Affairs Video Archives, 1992.

Perot, Ross. (10/20/92). "Perot Campaign Commercial," C-SPAN recorded Speech, Purdue University: Public Affairs Video Archives, 1992.

Ranney, Austin. *Channels of Power: The Impact of Television on American Politics.* New York: Basic Books, 1983.

Schnell, James A. "C-SPAN as a Database for Intercultural Communication," in Janette K. Muir, *C-SPAN in the Communication Classroom: Theory and Application.* Annandale, VA: Speech Communication Association, 1992.

Smith, Craig Allen. "The Interpretive Systems Approach to Teaching Political Communication," in Janette K. Muir, *C-SPAN in the Communication Classroom: Theory and Application.* Annandale, VA: Speech Communication Association, 1992.

Washington Post. July 12, 1992, 1 & A-10.

Chapter Two

Communication and Symbolism:
The Development of the Symbolic Event in American Culture

Definitions

rebellion—"open opposition to a person or thing in a position of authority or dominance" (*Webster's Third New International Dictionary*, 1961)

language—"any system of signs, symbols, etc. used for communication" (*American Heritage Dictionary*, 1976)
—"the vocabulary and phraseology belonging to an art or department of knowledge" (*Webster's Third New International Dictionary*, 1961)

event—"an occurrence or happening which produced consequences, or which creates personal and social structures that continue the life of the occur ence" (Evans, 654)

symbol—"something that stands for or suggests something else by reason of relationship, association" (*Webster's Third New International Diction ary*, 1961)

gesture—"anything said or done to convey a state of mind or intention" (*Web ster's Third New International Dictionary*, 1961)

sign—"a motion, gesture, or bodily action by which a thought is expressed or a command or a wish is made known" (*Webster's Third New International Dictionary*, 1961)

It is my contention that events are correlated with symbols, and gestures are correlated with signs. As an event "creates personal and social structures that continue the life of the occurrence," it also "stands for or suggests something else by reason of relationship." As a gesture is "anything said or done to convey a state of mind or intention," it also offers a means "by which a thought is expressed" and it "points to some reality outside of itself."

I purport that a symbolic event is comprised of signallic gestures. Application of this position, to the rebellion at Kent State University, reveals that the Kent State shootings are a symbolic event and that the symbolic event is comprised of signallic gestures. The purpose of this chapter will be to further develop this application.

On May 4, 1970, the Ohio National Guard shot into a crowd of students at Kent State University killing four and wounding nine. These shots not only ended four days of confrontation at Kent, they also symbolically ended a decade of violent antiwar protest. This decade of violence was felt throughout the country. Until Kent State, civil rights violence had been predominant in the south and antiwar violence had been felt in the east and west. Kent State served to "bring the war home" (a goal of the Students for Democratic Society) to the midwestern farmland of our country. The government and the antiwar movement went to school during those four days in May. The lesson acknowledged the momentum of the anti-war movement, the determination of the Guard, the price of violence over negotiation, and (perhaps most distinctly) . . . the guns are loaded.

During the civil unrest of the 1960s there were a large number of incidents that contained symbolic connotations of rebellion. There were many signs of rebellion, but the test of time has shown that there are few symbols of rebellion from that era. One such symbol is "Kent State." Contrast of Kent State with other signs of rebellion will better clarify this statement.

Throughout the 1960s the University of California at Berkeley was recognized as a bastion of student revolution. A primary occurrence that helped earn this reputation dealt with the Free Speech Movement in 1964. William O'Neill (1978) describes the situation in *Coming Apart: An Informal History of America in the 1960s.*

In September 1964 a University official ordered student activists to remove their literature tables from a strip of sidewalk before the campus main gate. . . . On September 29 four student groups set up tables in defiance of the ban. Tensions rose until on October 1 campus police arrested Jack Weinberg. . . . Students surrounded the police car, immobilizing it through the night. The administration then made a deal that took Weinberg off the hook. . . . Just when the crisis seemed over, the regents of the University renewed it (the ban). . . . On December 1 student leaders gave the regents 24 hours to drop their charges. When they didn't, students took over the administration building, Sproul Hall. (Mario) Savio gave his famous speech indicting the University as a machine that treated students as raw material. "It becomes odious, so we must put our bodies against the gears, against the wheels . . . and make the machine stop until we're free . . ." On December 3 a student strike took place. Perhaps more than half the University's classes did not meet. On December 7 President Clark Kerr spoke to 18,000 people in the outdoor Greek Theater. . . . Next day the faculty convened and, after a wild debate broadcast to students listening outside the auditorium, voted to place no restrictions on the content of speech or advocacy. The Free Speech Movement appeared to have won. (279-280)

During the first five months of 1968, the National Student Association counted 221 major demonstrations at 101 colleges and universities. O'Neill (1978) follows up on this discussion by describing the most crucial of these demonstrations.

But Columbia, by far the most spectacular, may stand for all the rest. . . . Columbia was an important landlord in Harlem, and was building a lavish gymnasium on city land adjoining the ghetto. Though neighborhood people were to have the use of separate facilities in it, militant black leaders remained dissatisfied. . . . On April 23 a mixed band of SDS (Students for Democratic Society) and the Students' Afro-American Society members marched on Low Memorial Library. Repulsed by guards, they went to the gymnasium site shouting "Gym Crowe Must Go," and they tore down a section of fencing. They then occupied Hamilton Hall, executive center of the undergraduate college. . . . There the young idealists ransacked President Grayson Kirk's files, drank his sherry, and smoked his cigars. In the next few days other buildings were taken and converted into "revolutionary communes," each with its own style and, sometimes, ideology. . . . Negotiations having failed, President Kirk ordered the police in early one morning (when Harlem would presumably be asleep) and the revolution was suppressed. About 700 students were arrested and 150 injured. (290)

Review of the incidents that occurred shortly before and after the Kent State shootings reveal the violence at Kent State was not an isolated occurrence. A week after the Kent State shootings, a similar protest and subsequent confrontation happened at Jackson State University in Mississippi. The shootings at Jackson State resulted in the death of two Black students. Bettina Aptheker (*Left Review*, 1980) provides an insight that begins to explain why the Jackson State shootings were only a sign (in comparison to the symbolic shootings at Kent State).

Black students battled police all over the South. They were arrested by the thousands, gassed, herded with cattle prods, and beaten. They were shot and killed at Tuskegee, Orangeburg, Texas Southern and Jackson State. The Student Non-Violent Coordinating Committee (SNCC) was one of the first national organizations in the United States to condemn the war in Vietnam, and SNCC initiated some of the first and most significant actions against the draft. The violence against Black students was reported, often lamented, even condemned. But it was expected. (3)

As previously mentioned, I view the Free Speech Movement, the takeover at Columbia, and the shootings at Jackson State as being significant, but they are not to be mistaken for symbolic events. Although the occurrences are significant, they have not "created personal and social structures that continue the life of the occurrence."

With this description serving as criteria for a symbolic event, the Kent State shootings do qualify as a symbolic event. The "life of the occurrence" has been continued in two primary areas. Each year since the shootings, there have been well-attended May 4 observances on the anniversary of the shootings. Classes have been cancelled on May 4 since 1978. Also, since the shootings, Kent State has been used as a forum for numerous activist concerns. S.R. Thulin (*Left Review*, 1980) writes "The May fourth movement is the logical expression of our common struggles against imperialism, militarism, and domestic oppression"

(2). The Kent Left Studies Forum has adopted the slogan "many struggles, many roads." Says Thulin, "For the spring of 1980, all roads lead again to Kent" (2).

Before analyzing Kent State as a symbol of rebellion, and recognizing the gestures which comprise the event, it is beneficial to lay a firmer base by reviewing various perspectives of the shootings. Senator Frank Church provides such a position (*Left Review*, 1980) by summing up a view maintained by many of his colleagues, "Kent State has become one of a number of synonyms that represent an era, a tragic event in the course of growing opposition to a misbegotten war 10,000 miles from home" (1).

From another end of the political spectrum, Frank Boehm (1971) comes to a parallel conclusion as the National Chairman of the Young Socialist Alliance. In the introduction of *May 1970: Birth of the Antiwar University*, Boehm writes "the Kent massacre showed the link between the endless slaughter of Indo-Chinese people and American troops in a hated war and the willingness of the government to turn its guns on those in this country who fight to end that war" (3). The notes from Susan Lamont's journal (Boehm, 1971), as National Secretary of the Young Socialist Alliance, provide further insight. "May 6, 1971—The Cambodian invasion and Kent State massacre have combined to trigger the largest, most extensive student strike the world has ever seen. In a number of schools, students, following votes in meetings of tens of thousands, have won direct control of campus facilities" (41).

In an article entitled "May 1970: Something Unprecedented in American History" (Boehm, 1971), Don Gurewitz deals with a fundamental issue which served to make the Kent State shootings a symbolic event.

> Previously they may have been able to say about the antiwar movement, "Well, those are hippies from the Haight," or whatever. But there are now millions and millions of people in this country who have to deal with the question of political activism around the issue of the war in very personal terms; in terms of their sons or daughters or nieces or nephews or friends. (53)

Nine years later, Bettina Apthecker (*Left Review*, 1980), perhaps with the advantage of time, provides a more conclusive summation of the relevance surrounding the shootings.

> Kent is a small town. It is in the industrial heartland of the United States. The students at Kent State are the sons and daughters of industrial workers and small townsfolk in middle America. Now even they were protesting the war. This was no radical fringe, no Black minority, no Communist zone of Eastern conspirators. This was Nixon's "silent majority." These were "his" folks. These were his troops, on his most trusted soil. (3)

Within this backdrop, indicating the significance of the Kent State shootings, we can further analyze the symbolic event by recognizing the signallic gestures which comprise it. This discussion is based upon a number of premises which were previously stated. To ensure a solid understanding, these premises will be reviewed.

The language ("any system of signs, symbols, etc. used for communication") being discussed is "rebellion." The study of rebellion reveals signs, symbols, etc., which have been used for communication. Within the language of rebellion, we are focusing on a particular symbolic event. Kent State is a symbolic event as it has "created personal and social structures that have continued the life of the occurrence" and it "stands for or suggests something else by reason of relationship." The symbolic event is comprised of signallic gestures; the individual signallic gestures being "anything said or done to convey a state of mind or intention" that "point to some reality outside of itself."

Analysis of the signallic gestures provide a chronological review of the symbolic event. Within this review, I will describe the symbolic event by using signallic gestures as fundamental indicators. The signallic gestures are in italicized print.

On April 30, 1970, President Nixon announced he was sending U.S. troops into Cambodia. This announcement contradicted previous statements by Nixon. He justified the invasion by saying such a move would aid in ending the war and that U.S. troops would be in Cambodia for less than six weeks.

The following day, Friday, May 1, *protestors buried a copy of the U.S. Constitution* by the Victory Bell on the commons. They claimed it had been "murdered" when President Nixon sent troops into Cambodia without the consent of Congress. During the rally, the *protestors claimed they were going to napalm a dog* to show the effects of napalm. (Napalm is an inflammatory mixture which was used as a weapon against Vietnamese.) Prior to the announced napalming, some uninvolved bystanders physically took the dog from the rally organizers to show they wouldn't allow such abuse on the Kent campus. At that time, the organizers used the dog abduction to show that "Kent students are more concerned with the life of a dog than they are with the lives of human beings in Vietnam." The rally served to perpetuate more antiwar feelings.

That evening, many students were in the downtown bar district of Kent. It was a warm spring night. Early in the evening, antiwar activists laid the groundwork for a small-scale riot on Water Street (the "main drag" of the bar district). A motorcycle gang showed up and performed stunts with their bikes as students cheered them on. The streets were blocked off. *Bonfires were set and eventually area businesses were vandalized.*

At around midnight, Kent's *Mayor Leroy Satrom proclaimed a state of civil emergency and ordered the bars closed immediately.* The crowd became a violent mob as angry drinkers filled the streets. Vandalism continued as police tried to disperse the gathering. The city of Kent was in need of police protection throughout the night.

The "trashing" of Water Street led to Mayor Satrom contacting Governor James Rhodes to request assistance from the Ohio National Guard. On the evening of Saturday, May 2, *the Guard entered the city of Kent.*

At dusk on Saturday, a crowd formed at the Victory Bell on the commons. The crowd eventually mobilized and marched throughout the campus . . . gaining support along the way. Within a couple of hours, *2,000-3,000 students surrounded the ROTC building and set it afire*. As the building burned out of control, protestors blocked attempts by local firefighters to put out the blaze. From that point, through the next four days, *the campus was in the hands of the Guard*.

On Sunday, May 3, students (who'd been gone for the weekend) returned to campus. It was a warm spring day and a deceptively festive mood prevailed with the presence of the uniformed visitors. During the afternoon, *Allison Krause placed a flower in the barrel of a guardsman's rifle* and asked him to pose for a picture. He flashed the "peace sign" with his free hand as the picture was taken. She was one of the four to die the following day.

Early in the day, Governor Rhodes visited the burned down ROTC building. During an afternoon press conference, Rhodes stated "we are going to eradicate the problem—we're not going to treat the symptoms." Rhodes emphasized that the university must remain open. During this period a rumor prohibiting the right of assembly began to spread throughout Kent.

On Sunday evening, students gathered at various places on campus. There was confusion surrounding the curfews that were in effect in Kent and on the campus. As the evening wore on, students peacefully protested the presence of the Guard. *Guardsmen eventually used tear gas to enforce the alleged prohibition of assembly*. Any good feeling between the Guard and students clearly went up in smoke.

Monday, May 4, was a day of confusion. Although the university remained open, there was an alleged prohibition of assembly being enforced. Faculty and students asked the question "are not classes a form of assembly?" At 11:00 a.m. a crowd of students gathered at the Victory Bell on the commons. It was a warm sunny day and other students were also on the commons . . . eating lunch, throwing frisbees, enjoying the sun, and watching the early stages of the noon rally. *The Guard was stationed around the burned down ROTC building*.

At noon, the students were ordered to disperse in accordance with the rumored prohibition of assembly. The Guard's dispersal order was ignored by the students and a few of the Guardsmen were pelted with rocks and obscenities as they ordered the students to disperse. Carrying loaded weapons, fixed bayonets, and firing tear gas, *the Guard proceeded to clear the commons*.

What happened during the next half hour has been the topic of much controversy and litigation. For the purpose of this chapter, I have no reason to speculate on the rationale used by the Guard or the students. It is sufficient to adhere to the confirmed facts. Between noon and 12:30 p.m., *the Guard shot into a crowd of students . . . killing four and wounding nine*.

Soon after the shootings *the university was closed down* and students were told to leave the campus immediately. It was the first of many campuses to close as a result of the shootings.

In *Rebellion in the University*, Seymour Lipset (1972) reflects on the impact of these occurrences. "The Cambodian events and the killings at Kent State and Jackson State resulted in the first national strike of long duration" (5). The course of happenings leading up to (and following) the shootings served to not only close universities nationwide, they also had a strong effect on public opinion. Lipset addresses such speculation.

The obvious question arises to what extent the events surrounding the Cambodian incursion, the killings at Kent State and Jackson State, and the mass involvement in the various forms of protest during May and June of 1970 increased the alienation from the American political system. . . . A Harris Survey conducted in late May reported that the confidence expressed in the President's Vietnam policy or in his general activities had almost totally vanished among students as a result of these events. (57)

In *May 1970: Birth of the Antiwar University*, Don Guerewitz (Boehm, 1971) provides a more extensive reaction to the shootings.

What happened in the last couple weeks is something unprecedented in American history. There was a whole vast social layer of the population—hundreds of thousands of youth—directly involved in a political struggle around one of the key political questions of our era, the imperialist war in Vietnam. (52)

The Picture

Immediately after the shots were fired, John Filo (a freelance photographer), using a borrowed camera, took pictures of the aftermath. One of these pictures showing a young girl kneeling over the dead body of Jeff Miller has been a memorable photograph through its depiction of the death and emotion that prevailed. This picture was carried on the cover of newspapers and magazines throughout the country and was frequently used on television when reference was made to the Kent shootings. The girl kneeling over Jeff Miller's body was Mary Veechio, a fourteen-year-old runaway from Opa Locka, Florida. She can be recognized as being representative of the climate at Kent State. A runaway, no home, frustrated with the system, unsure of where she was going . . . but doing her best to get there.

The Song

Soon after the shootings, Neil Young recorded and released a song about the shootings. It was simply titled "Ohio." The song captured the essence of the event, received considerable radio play, and had significant sales. The song was very popular in 1970 and was frequently a context song that was played in future years on anniversary reporting related to the shootings. It symbolically conveys much of the frustration and injustice associated with the shootings and conflicting forces that collided May 1-4.

The May 4 Observances

Since 1970, rallies have been held on May 4 in commemoration of the shootings. Although the rallies have varied in size and content, they have served as an annual gesture to recognize the meaning of May 4.

In the spring of 1977, the university approved plans for the construction of a gymnasium annex to be located on Blanket Hill, the area where the National Guard fired from in 1970. Opposition to the gym materialized as many people saw *the destruction of Blanket Hill as another means of covering up the 1970 shootings.*

Led primarily by the May 4 Coalition (founded on May 4, 1977), protestors began their occupation of Blanket Hill with the formation of a Tent City. With colleges letting out for the summer, students came from around the country to camp at Tent City.

An order to vacate Blanket Hill was submitted to the protestors. The *protestors refused to obey the order and police arrested 197 Tent City residents* as over 2,000 people watched. *The arrests went peacefully.* The Tent City had lasted sixty-three days.

Excavation of Blanket Hill began in September 1977. Construction continued without serious incident until September 24, when *over 3,000 protestors occupied the construction site,* damaging equipment in their dissent against the gym. The protest resulted in the *fencing of the site and a court order restricting trespass* into the area.

Construction continued on schedule until *another protest occurred on October 22.* After tearing down most of the fencing surrounding the area, the protestors were once again able to briefly occupy the construction site. The controversial construction continued within a few days. With most of the fencing torn down and a lot of the equipment damaged, *security was escalated and larger fences were erected.*

The contractor for the excavation of Blanket Hill was Bucky Arnes, a local subcontractor from Stowe, Ohio. *He flew an American flag over his construction trailer;* saying he was "working in the name of justice."

With the building of the gym underway, the 1978 May 4 commemoration carried more emphasis than in previous years. It began on the evening of May 3 with a candlelight march through the campus. *Joining in the procession was Kent State President Brage Golding. An all-night vigil was maintained* in the parking lot where the four students were killed.

The next day *a rally was held* on the Kent commons. Over fifteen speakers discussed May 4 related issues and also solicited support for other issues such as the "No Nukes" (anti-nuclear) movement. Throughout the rally, *riot police were stationed within the construction site.*

That afternoon the rally mobilized for a march through the campus and city. After the march, the rally converged on the construction site. *Governor Rhodes was burned in effigy* for his part in the shootings and subsequent cover-up attempts. Tear gas was eventually fired into the crowd, forcing the protestors back from the top of Blanket Hill.

In 1978, *George Segal was commissioned to create a sculpture commemorating the Kent State shootings.* Segal used the biblical theme of Abraham and Isaac" to depict the atmosphere in which the shootings took place. *The sculpture was eventually rejected by the university administration* due to its "violent overtones." Within a week, *the work was accepted by Princeton University.*

Another, less related, incident occurred in August of 1977 at the opening of the Ohio State Fair. During the opening day ceremonies, Steve Conliff, a member of the *Youth Independent Party (Yippies), hit Governor Rhodes with a banana cream pie.* The pieing was a result of, among other things, Governor Rhodes involvement with the Kent State shootings and Kent State cover-up. The direct significance of this incident is questionable, but it clearly stems from the Kent State controversy.

A more serious situation occurred for Rhodes in 1975 during a *civil damage lawsuit against Rhodes and twenty-seven National Guardsmen* for their part in the 1970 shootings. The suit was filed by the wounded and families of the slain. After a fifteen-week trial, *Rhodes and his fellow defendants were cleared of any guilt* in relation with the shootings.

In early 1978, *a retrial was ordered due to jury tampering* in the 1975 trial. The retrial was underway by that December. With the gym controversy still an issue, the Kent State analysis received considerable attention. A couple of weeks into the trial, a strong push was made by Rhodes to end the case with an out-of-court settlement. On January 4, 1979, eight years and eight months after the Kent State shootings, the *state approved a $675,000 out-of-court settlement* to the wounded and families of the slain. In addition, Governor Rhodes and the twenty-seven defendants signed the following *statement of concern.*

In retrospect, the tragedy of May 4, 1970 should not have occurred. The students may have believed that they were right in continuing their mass protest in response to the Cambodian invasion, even though this protest followed the posting and reading by the university of an order to ban rallies and an order to disperse. These orders have since been determined by the sixth Circuit Court of Appeals to have been lawful. Some of the Guardsmen on Blanket Hill, fearful and anxious from prior events, may have believed in their own minds that their lives were in danger.

Hindsight suggests that another method would have resolved the confrontation. Better ways must be found to deal with such confrontations. We devoutly wish that a means had been found to avoid the May 4 events culminating in the Guard shootings and the irreversible deaths and injuries. We deeply regret those events and are profoundly saddened by the deaths of four students and the wounding of nine others which resulted. We hope that the agreement to end this litigation will help to assuage the tragic memories regarding that sad day.

Pamphlet
"The May Fourth Site"
1980

Throughout the 1970s, Kent State served as a forum for various protest movements; movements which perpetuated national protest in the 1980s. As previously stated in this chapter, S.R. Thulin (*Left Review*, 1980) writes:

> The May Fourth movement is the logical expression of our common struggles against imperialism, militarism, and domestic oppression. . . . KLSF (Kent Left Studies Forum) pointed the way four years ago for local socialists in its first issue and Manifesto: "We embrace the ideal of solidarity, typified by the slogan 'Many struggles, many roads.'" For the spring of 1980, all roads lead to Kent. (2)

Conclusion

Using the terms and definitions provided, "Kent State" has been defined as a symbol of rebellion. This perspective acknowledges other parallel incidents (such as the Berkeley Free Speech Movement, Columbia University Student Strike, and the shootings at Jackson State University) as being signs of rebellion.

In developing this position, the "language" discussed was "rebellion." (Language being "any system of signs, symbols, etc., used for communication.") Within the language of rebellion, a particular symbolic event (Kent State) was focused upon. Kent State was recognized as a symbolic event as it has "created personal and social structures that have continued the life of the occurrence" and it "stands for or suggests something else by reason of relationship." This symbolic event was found to be composed of signallic gestures. Signallic gestures are defined as being "anything said or done to convey a state of mind or intention" that "point to some reality outside of itself." The signallic gestures, which comprise the symbolic event, have been recognized in such a way to create a chronological review of the symbolic event.

Notes

Adamek, R.J. and Lewis, J.M. "Social Control, Violence and Radicalization: The Kent State Case," *Social Forces*, March 1873, 342-347.

American Heritage Dictionary. New York: Dell Publishing Co., 1976.

Aptheker, B. *Left Review*. Kent, Ohio: Kent Popular Press, 1980.

"As Times Change, So Do Signs, Signals," *Smithsonian*, September 1976, 72-74.

Boehm, F. *May 1970: Birth of the Antiwar University*. New York: Pathfinder Press, 1971.

"Build Up To Tragedy at Kent State," *U.S. News and World Report*, May 25, 1970, 19.

Bryant, D. "Sowing the Wind, A Special Report From Kent State University," *Christianity Today*, June 5, 1970, 13-15.

"Coalition Member Disperses Crowd as Police Fail," *Cleveland Plain Dealer*, July 13, 1977, A-7.

"Costly Blessing at Kent State?" *Christian Century*, May 20, 1970, 620.

Davies, P. *The Truth About Kent State: A Challenge To American Conscience*. New York: Farrar, Straus & Giroux, 1973.

"Double Focus on Kent State: Findings of Grand Jury At Odds With Those of Scranton Commission," *National Review*, November 3, 1970, 1146.

"Eight Years Is Enough." *The Young Communist*, May 1978, 7.

Eszterhas, J. "Ohio Honors It's Dead," *Rolling Stone*, June 10, 1971, 14-18.

Eszterhas, J. *Thirteen Seconds: Confrontation at Kent State*. New York: Dodd, Mead, 1970.

Evans, J.C. "Symbol and Event," *Christian Century*, May 27, 1970, 653-654.

Evans, P. *The Protest Virus*. London: Pitman Publishing, 1974.

"Ex-Guardsman Arrested in Protest at KSU." *Cleveland Plain Dealer*, July 16, 1977, A-8.

"Freedom, Symbols, and Communication," *Annals of the American Academy*, March 1974, 11-20.

Furlong, W.B. "The Guardsmen's View of the Tragedy at Kent State," *The New York Times Magazine*, June 21, 1970, 12-13, 64, 68-69, 71.

Gallagher, T. "Tragedy At Kent State," *Good Housekeeping*, October 1970, 82-83.

"Handful of Yippies Disrupt Kent Commemoration." *Cleveland Plain Dealer*, May 5, 1978, A-4.

Hensley, T.R. and Lewis, J.M. *Kent State and May 4*. Dubuque, IA: Kendall/Hunt Publishing Co., 1978.

Hughes, H. *Crowd and Mass Behavior*. Boston: Allyn and Bacon, 1972.

"In the Aftermath of Kent State Indictments," *U.S. News and World Report*, November 2, 1970, 32-33.

"Investigations: The Kent State Case," *Newsweek*, May 25, 1970, 33-34.

Joy, T. "Kent State Eight Years After," *Student Lawyer*, November 1977, 25-30.

"Kent State: Another View," *Time*, October 26, 1970, 27.

"Kent State: What Happened: Contradictory Judgments Among the Three Reports," *Newsweek*, November 23, 1970, 32-33.

"KSU Annex, Once Resisted, Ready To Use." *Cleveland Plain Dealer*, August 30, 1977, A-8.

"KSU Coalition Readies to Continue Gym Halt In Court." *Cleveland Plain Dealer*, August 30, 1977, B-1.

"KSU Dean Warns Student Brigade of Future Protests." *Cleveland Plain Dealer*, October 14, 1977, A-8.

"KSU May Ask Court to Halt Coalition Rally." *Cleveland Plain Dealer*, October 21, 1977, A-15.

"KSU May 4 Coalition to Rally Nationwide." *Cleveland Plain Dealer*, July 13, 1977, A-7.

"KSU President Bars Coalition Rally." *Cleveland Plain Dealer*, October 20, 1977, A-14.

"KSU President Olds Attempts to Address Protestors." *Cleveland Plain Dealer*, July 7, 1977, A-9.

"KSU Trustees are Weighing Alternate Site." *Cleveland Plain Dealer*, August 21, 1977, 111.

"KSU Wants Total Ban on Some Rallies." *Cleveland Plain Dealer*, October 25, 1977, A-10.

Kunen, J.S. *The Strawberry Statement*. New York: Avon Books, 1968.

LeBon, G. *The Crowd*. New York: Viking Press, 1972.

"Legal Responsibility Still Disputed." *Daily Kent Stater*, May 4, 1978, 7.

Lewis, J.M. "A Study of the Kent State Incident Using Smelser's Theory of Collective Behavior," *Sociological Inquiry*, No. 2, 1972, 87-96.

Lewis, J.M. "Review Essay: The Telling of Kent State," *Social Problems*, Fall 1971, 267-279.

"Liberal Nostalgia at Kent Protests." *Young Spartacus*, May 1978, 3.

Lipset, S. *Rebellion in the University*. London: Pittman Publishing, 1972.

McGehee, E.G. "A Case of Civil Disobedience," *Christian Century*, December 28, 1977, 1217-1223.

"May 4 Coalition Turns Down Landscaping Changes." *Cleveland Plain Dealer*, August 20, 1977, A-19.

Maynard, Joyce. *Looking Back*. New York: Avon Books, 1972.

Meir, A. and Rudwick, E. "The Kent State Affair: Social Control of a Putative-Value Oriented Movement." *Sociological Inquiry*, No. 2, 1972, 81-86.

Michener, James. *Kent State: What Happened and Why*. New York: Random House, 1971.

"Mood of Unity Prevails During Peace March." *Daily Kent Stater*, May 4, 1978, 3.

"More Than People Died at Kent State," *Nation,* April 26, 1980, 492-494.

"My God! They're Killing Us." *Newsweek*, May 18, 1970, 31-33F.

"Need Compromise on New Gym Site." *Cleveland Plain Dealer*, June 8, 1977, B-2.

"New KSU Head Pledges Open Door." *Cleveland Plain Dealer*, June 10, 1977, A-9.

O'Neil, R.M. *No Heroes, No Villains*. San Francisco: Jossey-Bass, 1972.

O'Neill, William. *Coming Apart: An Informal History of America in the 1960s*. New York: Quadrangle Books, 1978.

"Oval Candlelight Rally Recalls 1970 Killings." *Ohio State University Lantern*, May 5, 1978, 1.

Park, R. *The Crowd and the Public*. Chicago: The University of Chicago Press, 1972.

Peterson, R.E. *Campus Aftermath of Cambodia and Kent State*. Berkeley, CA: Carnegie Foundation for the Advancement of Teaching, 1971.

"Portage Judge Bans Rallies at KSU." *Cleveland Plain Dealer*, October 22, 1977, A-5.

Reich, C.A. *The Greening of America*. New York: Bantam Books, 1970.

Report of the National Advisory Commission on Civil Disorders. New York: Bantam Press, 1968.

"Report of Kent State: Knight Newspaper Findings on Killing of Students," *Newsweek*, June 1, 1970, 67.

Sale, Kirkpatrick. *SDS*. New York: Vintage Books, 1973.

Shriver, P. *The Years of Youth: Kent State University 1910-60*. Kent, OH: Kent State University Press, 1960.

"Site Re-Occupied At Coalition Rally." *Daily Kent Stater*, September 27, 1977, 1, 3.

"Sit-In Ends as Demonstrators Demands Heard." *Cleveland Plain Dealer*, May 5, 1977, C-5.

Special Report: The U.S. President's Commission on Campus Unrest. New York: Arno Press, 1970.

"State Settles KSU Suit Out of Court, Pays $675,000; 'Apology' is Disputed." *Cleveland Plain Dealer*, January 5, 1979, A-1, A-12.

Stevens, M. and McGuigan, C. "Kent State Memorial," *Newsweek*, September 11, 1978, 99.

Stone, I.F. *The Killings at Kent State: How Murder Went Unpunished*. New York: Vintage Books, 1971.

"Tempo Changes, KSU Students React to Times." *Cleveland Plain Dealer*, May 25, 1979, A-18.

"The Beat Goes On." *Columbus Free Press*, October 5, 1977, 1, 7.

"The Future is Ours If We Dare To Take It." *Fight Back*, October 1977, 3, 19.

"The Rebellion of the Campus," *Newsweek*, May 18, 1970, 28-30.

"Student Rebellion: Vision of the Future or Echo From the Past?" *Political Science Quarterly*, June 1969, 289-310.

Thomkins, P. and Anderson, E.V. *Communication Crisis at Kent State*. Columbus, OH: Ohio State University Press, 1971.

Thulin, S.R. *Left Review*. Kent, Ohio: Kent Popular Press, 1980.

"Violence and Understanding: Campus Unrest and the Scranton Report," *Catholic World*, December 1970, 119-122.

Warren, W. *The Middle of the Country: The Events of May 4*. New York: Avon, 1970.

Webster's Third New International Dictionary. New York: World Publishing Co., 1961.

Chapter Three

Communication within the American Counterculture

During the 1960s a youth culture evolved which, among other things, tended to reject primary norms and values of the prevailing culture in favor of a more liberal lifestyle. This culture subsequently became known as the counterculture. Since that time, counterculture has taken on a number of meanings and is represented in various organizational structures.

Two primary explanations of counterculture are provided by Theodore Roszak, in *The Making of a Counterculture*, and Charles Reich, in *The Greening of America*. Roszak discusses counterculture as arising from a youthful revulsion at technocracy. It represents a refusal to surrender spontaneity to artificiality. The counterculture serves to reassert life and joy in the face of impersonal organization (Roszak, 1969, chapter 2).

Reich defines counterculture as arising from a perception by the young of contradiction between the stated ideals of the parental generation and their actual lifestyles. He designates six crises within this contradiction: disorder and corruption, decline of democracy, absence of community, poverty (in contrast with affluence), exploitation of technical resources (instead of expanding human resources), and a sense of loss of self (Reich, 1972, chapter 1).

To better understand counterculture, it is helpful to distinguish between subculture, contraculture, and counterculture. Cohen defines a subculture as "the existence, in effective interaction with one another, of a number of actors with similar problems of adjustment" (Cohen, 1955, 59). Within this situation new group standards are formed among the actors. In "Contraculture and Subculture," Yinger clarifies that subcultures can be recognized without intensive analysis of interaction with the larger culture (Yinger, 1960, 628-629). Yinger (1960) views contraculture as a subculture that stands in opposition to important aspects of the dominant culture. He suggests using the term contraculture:

> wherever the normative system of a group contains, as a primary element, a theme of conflict with the values of the total society, where personality variables are directly involved in the development and maintenance of the group's values,

and wherever its norms can be understood only by reference to the relationships of the group to a surrounding dominant culture. (629)

Counterculture is "a term used since the mid-1960s to describe a specific form of youth culture whose members reject key norms and values of the prevailing culture" ("Counterculture," 1974, 60). Counterculture is more readily recognizable, in contrast with subculture and contraculture, through its attempts to modify, change, and alter the dominant culture.

Woodstock is a small city located in the southeastern part of Midwestern State. Woodstock is a fictitious name. Pseudonyms have been used in the place of real names. Aside from being the county seat of Woodstock County, Woodstock is primarily known as the home of Midwestern State University. With 19,000 residents living in Woodstock and a student population of 14,000 the atmosphere is considerably tolerant of countercultural ideals in contrast with other cities and townships in that part of the state.

Within this tolerant atmosphere, a number of countercultural organizations evolved in Woodstock. One such organization was the Woodstock Food Cooperative (Co-op). The Co-op was initially started as a buying club which allowed members to order food in bulk once a month. As the buying club became established, it began the transition from a buying club to a Co-op, by renting space above a local restaurant for deliveries and purchases. After experiencing an increased cash flow, the buying club obtained a storefront and was recognized as a Co-op within the Federation of Orange River Co-ops (FORC).

Aside from the Co-op, there were other indicators of the countercultural tolerance in Woodstock during the period of the study. These indicators ranged from a variety of alternative organizations, such as SAFE (Safe Alternative Forms of Energy), People for Peace, Students for Peace, Woodstock Vietnam Veterans Against the War, and the Gay Rights Coalition, to the prevalent growth of high quality marijuana in the surrounding area.

The Woodstock Food Co-op was reflective of the alternative community that existed in Woodstock. The alternative atmosphere was frequently acknowledged in the Woodstock newspapers. The following is a quote from a local newspaper article about unique aspects of the community.

Woodstock occupies a special place in our hearts because it is a good place to cool out. Here one can live cheaply, ponder life's eternal mysteries and find plenty of people who won't question you about what you intend to do with your life. It's a good place to hide out. Outside of moving to Bhutan or Tasmania, there's no place one can become invisible faster than here. It's a good place to weird out. Short of conducting human sacrifices or advocating armed revolution, one will find a high degree of tolerance here. . . . Woodstock is one of the last places where the pleasant, relaxed ethos of the late 1960s still exists.

Problem

The problem of this study rests on the conflict resolution communication attempts practiced by the Woodstock Food Cooperative. I attempted to find if the primary ideals of the counterculture were evidenced in the communication attempts at conflict resolution. The Co-op presented itself as based on counterculture philosophy. I hypothesized the primary ideals of the counterculture would be evidenced in the communication attempts at conflict resolution.

I arrived at this hypothesis because I assumed there would be a trickle-down effect flowing from their core philosophies, through their organizational structures and on to their interpersonal communication. That is, I thought their unique philosophies would equate with unique forms on interpersonal relations. Conflict resolution communication is an area of organizational life and the resolution of conflict is an essential function carried out through interpersonal communication. Thus, I felt the primary ideals of the counterculture would be manifested in the communication attempts at conflict resolution.

The Co-op described itself as a "not-for-profit, good food, member-owned and democratically controlled business . . . membership is voluntary and open to all." A person could join the Co-op by paying a refundable twenty-dollar buying deposit. Members were owners and were encouraged to share in all aspects of the Co-op's operation. General business meetings were held the second Monday of each month.

The Co-op was managed through a committee system. The committees were Cashiers, Communications, Finance, Maintenance, Ordering, Orientation, and Receiving. Extended membership status was earned by individuals who were active with the Woodstock Birth Center, Woodstock World Hunger Coalition, People for Peace, and The Women's Collective.

Shopping at the Co-op was less formal than shopping at grocery stores. Members brought their own bags and containers for items packed in bulk, such as peanut butter, dried fruits, whole wheat pastas, beans, cooking oils, and liquid soaps. The underlying philosophy of the Co-op was that cooperation was a social, economic, and political idea about how people can work together to meet human needs. The introductory "Welcome" newsletter emphasized:

> Being a member means taking responsibility for yourself, and also for the building of a just, peaceful community and world. By operating the Co-op and buying from it, we seek to: 1) become part of an alternative, cooperative, not-for-profit economic system which practices consumer and producer ownership and control, 2) foster an ecologically sound food/production/distribution system, 3) educate consumers about food issues, 4) encourage local self-reliance.

In a Woodstock newspaper article entitled "Food store 'seed' of new society," Nick Hubbard (cashier) related, "It's an opportunity to not just be a food store, but to be part of an ideal to be the seed of a different society."

The Co-op manifested a number of functions that, when taken together, conveyed a unique environment. It was like a grocery store in that you could buy food there. It was like a classroom in that you could learn there. It was like a library in that you could buy books there. It was a community center in that you could socialize there or just simply hang out by yourself and watch the day go by. It was a goodwill center in that you could donate or seek free clothing and similar items there. It was a community bulletin board in that information was routinely posted there. The Co-op was very much a verb (implying a variety of ongoing activities) rather than a noun (that would be more likely to imply a place).

The Co-op was a unique concept but it was not unique insofar that there were many other Co-ops around the country at the time. If you were to travel to any university area you would have a good chance of finding a similar type of Co-op in existence. My experience was that the faces may be different but the characters were much the same. Thus, I felt comfortable focusing on this particular Co-op because it offered a representative picture of what life is like in such organizations. The behaviors and concerns expressed in this Co-op were duplicated in Co-ops across the United States. They may vary in size but the spirit was much the same.

The Co-op had roughly 200 active members during the period of the study. Active members were those who had paid their ten-dollar buying deposit. Approximately 40 of these 200 active members were consistently involved with the decision-making process within the Co-op. Such consistent involvement was generally exercised through employment as a cashier, committee work, or regular attendance at general membership meetings. The store was operated through consensus, whereby all members (present at monthly membership meetings) had to agree with new policies and amendments to the operating rules. The Co-op described itself as an egalitarian organization, whereby all members had equal power.

The consensus process was the decision-making and conflict resolution method used by the Co-op at monthly membership meetings. The primary appeal of consensus process was that it promoted cooperation instead of competition. It is a sixteen-step process that emphasizes discussion and compromise. The FORC organization also operated with consensus decision making. It was not-for-profit and democratically controlled. FORC, comprised of one representative per Co-op, met one weekend every two months. Any Co-op member was welcome to attend.

Within its "Bylaws, Structure, and Philosophy" FORC clarified its purpose and intent:

> FORC views itself as a part of a larger social and political movement directed towards creating a society which holds as its first principle the welfare of all human beings. We are a revolutionary organization and, as such, feel solidarity with other people and groups equally committed to providing people with the knowledge and resources necessary to control their own lives.

Method

I had two periods of contact with the Woodstock countercultural community. The first was a seventeen-month period between 1979 and 1981 in which I lived in the community and participated with the Co-op as a member. The second period, between March, 1981 and March, 1982, was spent doing fieldwork research in the Woodstock community and particularly at the Woodstock Food Co-op.

Zelditch (1970, 220) classifies field methods into three broad classes which he defines as being primary:

> Type I. Participant Observation. The fieldworker observes and also participates in the same sense that he has durable social relations in the social system.
> Type II. Informant Interviewing. We prefer a more restricted definition of the informant than most fieldworkers use, namely that he be called an "informant" only where he is reporting information presumed to be factually correct about others rather than about himself.
> Type III. Enumeration and Samples. This includes surveys and direct, repeated, countable observations.

I gathered data through participant observation, interviews, two surveys, and a review of literature written by/about the Co-op.

Participant observation was the main method used for data gathering. As a member of the Co-op, I had direct access to a variety of organizational situations. Access to the Co-op was exercised in five areas: general business meetings, working at the Co-op, working on three committees, involvement with Co-op-related social functions, and informally "hanging out" at the Co-op.

Informative interviews were conducted with members, and former members, of the Co-op. I sought to interview individuals who represented the variety of positions and perspectives maintained by the Co-op membership. Two surveys were used in the gathering of data. I administered a survey that involved processes in formal and informal settings, and the Co-op Orientation Committee (of which I was a member) administered a survey regarding the management of the Co-op. The Co-op printed monthly newsletters, handouts, submitted articles to the FORC newspaper, and had articles written about it in the Woodstock area newspapers. I reviewed this literature for information related to the research problem.

Peacock (1968, 270) discusses the use of a second observer in field research settings. I utilized the observations of a second observer to compare and contrast against my own observations.

Analysis of conflict resolution communication attempts was divided between formal settings (meetings) and informal settings (outside of meetings). Although the study was concerned primarily with conflict resolution communication attempts, I analyzed the lifestyles and value structures of the Co-op membership to provide additional perspective for the findings.

Findings

The data gathered during the period of the study indicated the Co-op conflict resolution communication attempts were based on a counterculture philosophy on the organizational behavior level, but the Co-op conflict resolution communication attempts exemplified dominant culture approaches on the core philosophy level. Organizational behaviors included elements such as rituals, procedures, clothing styles, jargon, and norms.

The Co-op usually used a form of voting within the consensus process framework, instead of using the actual process. That is, if no member opposed a proposal strong enough to give a major objection, then the proposal passed. A major objection is an irreconcilable objection to a proposal. It stops current action on the proposal and the major objector accepts responsibility for meeting with the proposer to rewrite the proposal. Power was generally based on who had information and position. If a proposal was objected against at a monthly membership meeting, the major objector and the proposer were supposed to work out an agreement on the objected proposal so it could be put on the agenda of the next monthly membership meeting.

The egalitarian ideals advocated by the Co-op were only superficially evident. Egalitarian ideals were evident on the organizational behavior level, but not on the core philosophy level. Egalitarian ideals were evident within Co-op rituals, procedures, clothing styles, jargon, and norms, but the egalitarian ideals were not recognized as genuine on the core philosophy level. The Co-op presented itself as egalitarian, but my analysis found consistent behavior contradictory to egalitarian ideals.

Member participation was correlated to power within the Co-op. A basic progression was participation with the organization that led to knowledge of the organization, which in turn led to referent power within the organization. A typical example of this progression was evidenced in the cashiers position at the Co-op. As cashiers, they participated considerably in the operation of the Co-op. This participation enhanced their knowledge about the functioning of the organization. As knowledgeable members, they were frequently referred to for advice or direction regarding the needs of the Co-op. Such consistent reference by the general membership established the cashiers in positions of power because they, more than most members, knew what was going on.

The degree to which a member could be identified with by other members was correlated with that member's position within the Co-op hierarchy. That is, if Co-op members did not identify with an individual member, this negatively affected that member's position of power and influence.

Burnout generally occurred when members became overinvolved with the Co-op and felt a need to withdraw from such involvement. Burnout did not represent disagreement or disenchantment with the Co-op; rather, it represented an interest to apply one's time and energy in another area. It was not uncommon for an individual to withdraw from the Co-op and then reinitiate involvement at a later date. Burnout affected the Co-op on three levels: temporary burnout at meetings, burnout experienced by an individual member, and burnout experienced by the entire organization.

Temporary burnout generally occurred near the end of monthly membership meetings. That is, members were tired of sitting and discussing and were anxious to leave. Earl Sebastian described how Rolf Haenisch, the former coordinator of the Co-op, used temporary burnout to his advantage. "He'd wait until the end of meetings, when everybody was burned out, and then propose stuff and give substantiation for the ideas, and folks generally went along with what he did." The coordinator was a temporary position which had been held only by Rolf.

The Co-op did not have an official constitution and bylaws, and subsequently experienced difficulty with recurring problems. A review of meeting minutes and newsletters from the Co-op evidenced problems which were dealt with, but which also managed to recur as problems. The Co-op appeared to "go in circles" with some problems.

Sixty-eight separate issues were analyzed during the period of the study. Typical issues were selected from my field notes to enhance a better understanding of fewer issues, as opposed to a weaker understanding of all the issues. Typical issues were those that were representative of behavior and phenomena consistently recognized during the period of the study. Each of the selected typical issues was classified according to the setting they occurred in, formal or informal, and the level of controversy which occurred, high or low level. Thus, there were four quadrants: high-level controversy issues in formal settings, high-level controversy issues in informal settings, low-level controversy issues in formal settings, and low-level controversy issues in informal settings. Formal settings were limited to monthly membership meetings and committee meetings. Informal settings included all situations other than Co-op monthly membership meetings and committee meetings.

The distinction between high-level controversy issues and low-level controversy issues was more arbitrary. I viewed all issues as being on one continuum regarding controversy and worked to recognize them for the degree of controversy they represented within the organization. Thus, issues representing a higher degree of controversy were classified as high-level controversy issues and issues representing a lower degree of controversy were classified as low-level controversy issues.

Aside from the setting in which issues occurred, distinctions were also recognized according to the types of issues. There were four types of issues: issues of logistics, issues of finance, issues of principle, and issues of personality. Issues of logistics involved the physical maintenance and day-to-day management of the Co-op. Issues of finance involved organizational expenses and the distribution of funds. Issues of principle involved ethical questions and the interpretation of the Co-op's philosophical base. Issues of personality involved the differences between members within the Co-op. The issues of each quadrant were subdivided according to these classifications, regarding issue types.

Table 1 outlines the four quadrants of conflict resolution which existed within the Co-op. The types of issues which existed within the quadrants are listed and the number of specific issues, which occurred under each type of issue heading are indicated. Examples of typical issues that were selected from my field notes will be described to exemplify previously stated findings. The examples of such issues represent each of the four quadrants.

Table 1
Four Quadrants of Conflict Resolution Attempts

	Formal Settings	Informal Settings
High-Level Controversy	Issues of Logistics: 2 Issues of Finance: 3 Issues of Principle: 7	Issues of Principle: 5 Issues of Personality: 5
Low-Level Controversy	Issues of Logistics: 7 Issues of Finance: 13 Issues of Principle: 6	Issues of Logistics: 4 Issues of Finance: 3 Issues of Principle: 10 Issues of Personality: 3

High-Level Controversy in Formal Settings

A typical issue in this quadrant involved Operation Wake-up. Operation Wake-up was conceived as a means to perpetuate revenues, community relations, and member involvement. The implementation of Operation Wake-up required the hiring of a coordinator to work on these goals. The membership was cautious in creating such a position because we did not know if we could afford it or if we wanted to get in the habit of paying members, other than cashiers, to do work.

Clark Yost introduced the idea at a store meeting. The store meetings were held a week before the monthly membership meetings; the purpose was to construct an agenda for the monthly membership meeting. The store meetings usually had about seven to eight members in attendance.

Clark proposed that the Co-op hire him as a member-coordinator to work four hours a week to "keep things going." He would be paid the same as cashiers. Drew Salzgaber replied "No, no, no, no, I'll major object to that all the way. . . . That's why I formed Outreach (a committee to gain new members). . . . " Clark and Drew stayed after the meeting and worked out their differences on the proposal for two hours. This process involved discussion, compromise, and eventual agreement. They entitled it Operation Wake-up. As implied in the title, the intent was to prompt the membership with this boost of enthusiasm.

An ad appeared in the Woodstock News the following week. "Attention all Woodstock Food Co-op members!! Your presence is needed at January's general meeting. . . . Proposal for Operation Wake-up!" Drew paid for the ad with money he borrowed from Clark. I talked with Lois, a cashier, about the ad. As I explained the proposal she interrupted me with the statement, "I think Clark just wants a job."

The proposal was formally reviewed at the end of the January 1982 monthly membership meeting. The meeting was moving into its third hour and Clark suggested a five-minute break. Ten minutes into Clark's description of the proposal, members started to put their coats on to leave. Randy Horn-Bestel: "I'm leaving in five minutes." Earl Sebastian: "A lot of us have got fires to bank" (wood-burning stoves). Clark realized there was not enough time to deal with the proposal and he suggested we form an ad hoc committee to refine the idea.

The ad hoc committee of eight members met ten days later to refine Clark's proposal. The first action was to define our goal as an ad hoc committee. We discussed and decided it dealt with the new job description and the future direction of the Co-op. Throughout the meeting, Clark Yost promoted ideas that represented structure and Allison Frye promoted ideas representing less structure. Allison: "We need more spirit and less structure." Allison got her way most of the time. The ad hoc committee members tended to identify with Allison as a person more than with Clark. This identification was fairly overt in some cases and less overt in other situations.

The Operation Wake-up proposal was on the February 1982 monthly membership meeting agenda. There were twenty-five minutes of discussion regarding the direction of the Co-op and the idea of hiring a coordinator. Earl Sebastian was a primary supporter of the proposal and he was also informally acting as facilitator when the issue was presented for consideration.

Earl: "This will be a historical move. The Co-op seems to have a historical move like this every few years. People are usually scared as hell but we usually end up bettering ourselves, it's how we've progressed. . . . In the past we combined buying clubs into a main Co-op, moved the Co-op to various locations, and eventually got our present store front. This is our next historical step. It's scary and it's exciting." Clark: "Yesterday's visionary will be tomorrow's general manager. Yesterday's movement will be tomorrow's system."

Earl then pushed for consensus. "Are there any major objectors?" We did not use the steps of the consensus process at all. There was no major objection and the proposal passed. A hiring committee was formulated and we met a week later to decide upon a hiring procedure. Interested members filled out applications and the applications were reviewed by the committee. Clark Yost was hired as the coordinator of Operation Wake-up. This issue was an issue of finance.

Low-Level Controversy in Formal Settings

Typical issues in this quadrant included extending the Saturday hours of operation and being open on Sundays. Janet Krebs proposed at the October 1981 monthly membership meeting that the Co-op extend Saturday evening closing time from 5 p.m. to 7 p.m. Store hours had been 11 a.m. to 5 p.m. There was a five-minute discussion among the cashiers regarding how busy the Co-op was on Saturdays. The rest of the membership listened to the discussion, but provided no input. A friendly amendment was submitted by the cashiers which suggested the Co-op be open from 10 a.m. to 6 p.m. on Saturdays. There were no objections. The amended proposal passed.

A suggestion that the Co-op be open on Sunday was listed as a discussion topic at the same meeting. The cashiers believed that Sunday would not be a very busy day and the best approach might be to use volunteer cashiers. That is, do not pay the members who volunteer as cashiers on Sundays. The cashiers said they would take an informal poll of members to see if there was interest in the idea.

Tom Kocher attended the November 1981 store meeting and suggested we discuss being open on Sunday at the monthly membership meeting. Tom: "When we first got started, Sunday was the only day we were open." We put it on the agenda, but the monthly membership meeting lasted too long and we did not have time to discuss the idea.

Tom Kocher resubmitted the proposal at the February 1982 store meeting. He led the discussion of the proposal at the following monthly membership meeting. He suggested we be open four hours on Sunday and use volunteer cashiers. Janet Krebs (a cashier) questioned the capability of volunteer cashiers. Janet: "This is a real business, we can't open the doors with anybody behind the counter representing us." Suggestions were made during the discussion and the membership decided the proposal should be modified and presented at the next meeting. The suggestions dealt with who should work and when they would work. The proposal was never brought up again and Tom Kocher did not attend any more Co-op meetings during the period of the study. These issues were issues of logistics.

High-Level Controversy in Informal Settings

Typical issues in this quadrant included expressed differences between Drew Salzgaber and Clark Yost, Drew Salzgaber and Nick Hubbard, and Drew Salzgaber and Adam Young. The following field note excerpts outline Clark's negative feelings about Drew.

> Met Karla Donaho in Lowell Center (university student center) to watch the evening news on television before going to the monthly membership meeting. Karla: "Clark is gonna tell Drew he doesn't wanna talk with him about the Co-op after the meetings are over from now on."

(After a store meeting a group of members were going drinking at the Shack.) Clark to Drew: "I'm personally inviting you not to come with us to drink beer tonight . . . 'cos I wanna talk with these folks without you."

Clark approached Karla and I to talk about Drew. He and others want to initiate action to terminate Drew's membership. . . . Clark: "Drew has been perpetuating a lot of negative energy and bad consciousness for a long, long time."

Clark was generally concerned with Drew's irresponsibility as a member of the Co-op and how this affected the image of the Co-op. Nick Hubbard (head cashier) seemed to represent the general views of the Co-op membership in his differences with Drew. That is, Nick's concerns with Drew usually involved Drew's violation of Co-op rules or instances when Drew's behavior was detrimental to Co-op discussions. His statements to Drew reflected appeals that Drew modify his behavior in the best interest of the Co-op. The following field note excerpts exemplify typical statements by Nick to Drew. These excerpts reveal the nature of their, at times strained, relationship.

Before the meeting started, Nick pulled Drew aside. Nick: "Come here Drew, I wanna talk with you a minute. This is a personal comment, not an official comment. You've got to quit talking so long during meetings and wasting so much time with stuff that isn't pertinent."

(At the Co-op). Nick: "Get off the phone Drew!!! Go use the pay-phone!" Drew: "I haven't got a dime." Nick: "Go to Lowell Center (to use their phones)." Drew: "I'll get arrested; I'm banned from there because of some crazy disagreement." Nick: "Well, you know the rules." Drew was not allowed to use the Co-op phone due to his previous unpaid long distance calls.

Drew came into the Co-op to use the phone. Nick was visibly upset. Nick: "No! You can't use the phone!" Drew: "Just one more time for an emergency." Nick: "Ya know Drew, there's a lot of people who wanna kick you out of the Co-op." Drew: "But I haven't done anything wrong." Nick: "The uneasy sentiment should serve as an indicator."

Clark and Drew were discussing Operation Wake-up at the Co-op and Drew seemed to disagree with everything Clark said. Nick yelled from behind the cash register: "You're a talker Drew, but you don't do a damn thing. You're a philosopher with no follow through. . . . If I had my way, well, never mind." Nick walked over to the booth where Clark and Drew were sitting. Nick: "You don't do a damn thing. All you do is talk."

Nick Hubbard and Clark Yost exercised considerable tolerance with Drew, but they did vent their frustrations periodically. The following situation occurred when I was administering the Co-op survey at the Co-op. Ironically, it was during that period I observed an atypical physical threat at the Co-op. It occurred without warning.

Drew wrote a ninety-dollar check to a friend of Adam Young's for a chainsaw. Adam's friend "really needed the money" and the check bounced. Adam approached Drew about the bounced check and Drew claimed it was a mistake. Adam told Drew he was gonna go with him to Adam's friend's house to straighten things out. Adam went to call his friend and told Drew "if you try to run out of here, I'll beat the crap out of you. I'm basically a nonviolent person but you stole from a friend of mine."

Drew is mentioned many times in my field notes. He is referenced in fifty-nine separate instances. Oddly enough, a majority of the membership had differences with Drew, but he rarely had differences with them. That is, I never observed a situation where Drew was criticizing another member, although he did criticize ideas. Rather, he was always in a defensive position being criticized by other members. These issues were issues involving differences of personality.

Low-Level Controversy in Informal Settings

A typical issue in this quadrant involved moving a cooling unit. I first learned of the issue involving the cooler while working with the maintenance committee. We were painting the Co-op floor on a Sunday when the Co-op was closed. I noticed a produce cooler that had never been used at the Co-op and asked Randy Horn-Bestel, the maintenance committee chairperson, about it.

Randy told how the cooler, Nick Hubbard's idea, was obtained and moved against the west wall. Since the move put the cooler under the heater, they decided to move it over to the east wall. After they moved it to the east wall, they found out the cooler should be by a window and would have to be moved back to the west wall. Since Randy helped move the cooler before, he would not help move it back to the west wall. Randy: "Somebody should get their act together with it."

Drew was talking with some other members, a month later, about grandiose plans for expanding the Co-op and there was a discussion about the Co-op's potential. Nick commented "Hell, we can't even get the cooler moved to the other side of the Co-op and we're talking about this other stuff." The cooler was never moved or used during the entire period of the study. This issue was an issue of logistics.

Conclusions

The Co-op conflict resolution communication attempts exemplified dominant culture attempts on the core philosophy level. The Co-op used voting within a consensus process framework in formal settings and a hierarchy was evident in informal settings. The Co-op conflict resolution communication attempts exemplified counterculture attempts on the organizational behavior level. Organizational behaviors included ritual, procedures, clothing styles, jargon, and norms. The Co-op presented itself, through organizational behaviors, as using the consensus process in formal settings, but analysis found it did not use the consensus process. The entire process was never used during the period of the study. The Co-op presented itself, through organizational behaviors, as an egalitarian organization in informal settings, but analysis found it did not practice egalitarian ideals.

These findings carry implications with the Dramaturgical school of symbolic interaction. That is, social interaction is based on the management of impressions we receive from each other. Erving Goffman (1959) develops this notion in *The Presentation of Self in Everyday Life*.

> I have said that when an individual appears before others his actions will influence the definition of the situation which they have come to have (6). When an individual appears before others he will have many motives for trying to control the impression they receive of the situation (15). In consequence, when an individual projects a definition of the situation and thereby makes an implicit or explicit claim to be a person of a particular kind he automatically exerts a moral demand upon the others, obliging them to value and treat him in the manner that persons of his kind have a right to expect (13).

The significance of the conflict resolution communication attempts is that the attempts constructed a presentation made by the organization members. A key importance of this presentation is that it impacted their self-perception, as an organization, and also impacted the perception that others had of their organization.

The Co-op presented itself as using the consensus process, which exemplifies counterculture ideals, but analysis found it did not use the consensus process. The Co-op presented itself as egalitarian, which exemplifies counterculture ideals, but analysis found it did not practice egalitarian approaches. Thus, the Co-op presented itself as countercultural through its conflict resolution communication attempts, and such attempts were often perceived as countercultural, but my analysis found the presentation of countercultural conflict resolution communication attempts to be superficial. That is, the countercultural ideals were only superficially evident through organizational behaviors.

The Co-op usually used voting within a consensus process framework in formal settings. The informal hierarchy was based on power by identification and participation. Participation within the organization led to knowledge about the functioning of the organization, which in turn led to referent power within the organization.

As I reviewed the data I was struck at how consistent the data reinforced the aforementioned finding and how blind I had been to this reality prior to engaging in formal study of the phenomena. I had been operating with the false assumption that what appeared to be radically different mindsets (between the dominant culture and counterculture) would be strongly reflected in a variety of organizational practices and communication processes on the interpersonal and group levels.

Such a finding is not huge but it is meaningful. It has helped me to exercise more scrutiny with impressions and assumptions I maintain about various groups and individual practices within such groups. This has been a benefit to me personally and professionally.

There was a considerable ideological and logistical distance between counterculture organizations and dominant culture organizations in the United States during the late 1960s and early 1970s. The past three decades have seen this distance become smaller with the formation of a common ground between counterculture organizations and dominant culture organizations. An example of this common ground was recognized, during the period of the study, when FORC adopted a Board of Directors and large supermarket chains gave increased emphasis to the marketing of health foods. That is, a Board of Directors approach was previously considered to be unacceptable in the counterculture and the health food market was not previously emphasized by the large, dominant culture, supermarket chains.

I believe the counterculture offers a needed alternative for those who reject the dominant culture. If the Co-op is representative of most countercultural organizations, counterculture ideals will only be superficially evident within most countercultural organizations. Could similar dichotomies exist within other types of dominant culture organizations? During the time of this study I recognized an example of such a dichotomy when I observed that the Strategic Air Command, formerly a major command of the U.S. Air Force, had adopted the motto "Peace is our Profession." Though peace through deterrence was an aspect of the Strategic Air Command it was more widely known for the nuclear arsenal it possessed.

I believe it would be beneficial to observe positions presented by various types of organizations through their organizational behaviors and compare the professed positions against their actual practices. Such analysis might reveal consistencies and trends that are reflective of our larger culture and, hence, also reflected in communication practices on the interpersonal level. The root of this finding could be grounded in a contradiction between how we perceive ourselves, individually and collectively, and what we actually are (based on our actions).

A long-term objective of such analysis might be that organizations could learn to assess themselves in this regard, thus avoiding outside inquiries and making it less threatening, and be able to adjust their actions accordingly so their actions will be more commensurate with their stated intentions. Or, at a minimum, their stated intentions could be adjusted to fit organizational practices. Thus, this type of inquiry could have short-term, intermediate-term, and long-term benefits. As such, the analysis described in this study is intended as a contribution towards the aforementioned types of benefits.

Notes

Cohen, Albert. *Delinquent Boys.* Glencoe, IL: Free Press, 1955.

"Counterculture." *Encyclopedia of Sociology*. Guilford, CT: Dushkin Publishing Group, Inc., 1974.

Goffman, Erving. *The Presentation of Self in Everyday Life*. Garden City, NY: Anchor Books, 1959.

Peacock, James. *Rites of Modernization*. Chicago: University of Chicago Press, 1968.

Reich, Charles. *The Greening of America*. New York: Random House, Inc., 1972.

Roszak, Theodore. *The Making of a Counterculture*. Garden City, NY: Anchor Books, 1969.

Yinger, J. Milton. "Counterculture and Subculture," *American Sociological Review*, No. 25 (1960), 625-635.

Zelditch, Morris. "Some Methodological Problems of Field Studies," in *Qualitative Methodology*, William Filstead, ed., Chicago: Markham Publishing Co., 1970, 217-231.

Chapter Four

An Analysis of the May 4, 1970, Kent State Shootings Using Smelser's Theory of Collective Behavior

On May 4, 1970, the Ohio National Guard shot into a crowd of students at Kent State University, killing four and wounding nine. These shots not only ended four days of confrontation at Kent, they also symbolically ended a decade of violent antiwar protest. This was a decade of violence that was felt throughout the country. Until Kent State, civil rights violence had been predominant in the south and antiwar violence had been felt in the east and west. Kent State served to "bring the war home" to the heart of the country. This was a goal of the Students for Democratic Society (SDS). The government and the antiwar movement went to school during those four days in May. Highlights of the lesson evidenced the momentum of the antiwar movement, the determination of the Guard, the price of violence over negotiation, and (perhaps most distinctly) the guns are loaded.

Kent State, apart from other antiwar violence, provides a unique instance of social contagion. Social contagion evolves from a rapid and irrational growth of a mood or impulse whereby rumors spread fast, actions are dictated by group impulse, and spectators become involved in the wave of activity. This was not a case where violent, drug-crazed, communist sympathizers were gunned down by rationally thinking National Guardsmen. The roles are not defined that clearly. Rather, in the course of May 1-4, there are many examples where social contagion served to label participants in roles that were not theirs. Sometimes, they were labeled in roles that were at the opposite end of the antiwar spectrum.

There were 113 Guardsmen in the contingent that worked to clear the Kent Commons prior to the shootings. In reviewing the backgrounds of these Guardsmen, there are cases where individuals joined the Guard due to pacifistic attitudes toward the war in Vietnam. The traditional "war monger" label given to men in uniform was far from true. Thus, in the midst of the Kent State social contagion, there were pacifists shooting at pacifists.

Bill Schroeder was a ROTC cadet on full scholarship. Before coming to Kent he'd been an all-state basketball player from Lorain, Ohio. On Monday, May 4, he went to see the remains of the burned down ROTC building. An antiwar rally had been scheduled for noon on the Commons. The students (some eating lunch, some there for the rally, some on their way to class, etc.) were ordered to disperse from the area. In less than an hour, the confusion would leave permanent effects. Bill Schroeder was 382 feet away from the Guardsmen that killed him.

In this irony, a pacifist (in uniform) is shooting at an ROTC cadet. As I remember it some called it justice, some called it murder, and others weren't quite sure what to call it. The passing of time allows us to interpret it as a case of social contagion.

Collective Behavior

The activities at Kent State clearly fall within the parameters of collective behavior. With Guardsmen and curfews on campus, the student gatherings developed in response to the problematic situations that arose. The collective behavior at Kent differed from mere social behavior in the following ways. It was less inhibited and more changeable; the crowd was spontaneous and open to action in various directions. (During the Friday night violence, preceding the Monday shootings, protestors temporarily changed directions when they helped police rescue a utility worker who nearly fell to the ground while working on a traffic light.) Due to a lack of concrete organization, most of the crowds at Kent were short lived; constantly dissolving and regrouping in various forms.

The Student Protestor

The student protestor can best be recognized by acknowledging his or her set of values. Although there are many to recognize, the value structure can be outlined through definition of key concepts. "Romanticism" relates to the ambition of knowing and experiencing all things (a romantic ideal). Opposition to arbitrary rules and regulations stems from "antiauthoritarianism." "Populism" emphasizes that the real power should rest with the masses (not the elite) and "antidogmatism" stresses opposition to the establishment. Opposition to actions that benefit one individual at the expense of others is underscored through appeals of "moral purity." "Anti-institutionalism" is closely aligned with antiauthoritarianism. It deals with distrust of society's conventional institutions such as business corporations, the military, and the church. Underlying all of this is a concern with "community and communication." This concern emphasizes human relationships, feelings, and emotions.

This set of values applies to the collective behavior of the student protestors. As individuals, many of the students may have disagreed with some of the aforementioned aspects. From a collective perspective though, these values can be recognized in the organized student groups and in the actions of such crowds.

The antiwar protests of the 1960s consisted of various levels of involvement from the protestors. The SDS was an organization that planned antiwar protests and worked to shape collective behavior and the direction of social contagion. In doing so they recognized three categories of protestors: the organizers (5 percent), the superintellectuals (5-10 percent), and the shock troops (85-90 percent). The organizers and the superintellectuals were involved with the groundwork of organizing and giving the SDS protests direction. The shock troops were less informed of specifics, and basically were hanging onto the abstract set of values previously mentioned. Thus, when the social contagion spread, it had little effect on the organizers or the superintellectuals, as they were more aware of what was happening. It was the shock troops that were beaten and arrested, rather than the instigators.

Even though the May 4 protest at Kent State wasn't organized by SDS, the same theory applies. None of the people killed or wounded were involved with planning or leading any of the protests.

Types of Crowds

Between 10:45 a.m. and 12:45 p.m. on May 4, the Kent Commons saw various levels of crowd participation. From 10:45 a.m. until 11:15 a.m., a casual crowd existed on the Commons. Many students were either coming from their ten o'clock class or were going to their eleven o'clock class. In doing so, the number of people on the Commons expanded and contracted (formed and dissolved) in the course of twenty minutes. Since the Commons is located in the center of the campus, this casual crowd process would occur eight or nine times a day.

A conventionalized crowd, much like an audience, began forming at about 11:15 a.m. As the day's activities continued, the conventionalized audience could be seen cheering and applauding the active protestors. This spectator group ranged from townspeople, to high school students, to professors and university students.

The acting crowd formulated by 11:50 a.m. The primary topic in morning classes, regardless of the course subject, dealt with the Guard's presence on campus. Thus, when the eleven o'clock classes ended, many students would go to the Commons. The acting crowd consisted of many types of students. Some were there to protest, some were there for lunch, and some were just on their way to class. Regardless of the reason, many of them got "caught up" in the acting crowd during the confusion following the dispersal order given by the Guard. Thus, the acting crowd started with an attention-getting event (the dispersal order), grew restless when they weren't sure what to do, and became more aware of the excitement that was occurring. At this point the active crowd responded to the contagion. They were open to action, shared a common goal, and were ready to act with unity.

By 12:05 p.m., the expressive crowd had collected. The confusion was heightened when the Guard fired tear gas and began physically dispersing the crowd. It was much like an acting crowd, except the tension served to cloud the goal or objective. The tension built. It was eventually released in physical activity . . . yelling, running, and throwing rocks. This slight relief served to create a feeling of exhilaration amongst the expressive crowd, especially when they were able to hinder the approaching Guardsmen. At the height of this experience, the feeling can be attached to persons or objects. Such is the case with the pagoda which stands in the middle of the Commons. Since the confrontation, the pagoda has served as a symbol of the Kent State shootings. The Guard was standing underneath and beside the pagoda as they fired into the crowd of protestors.

With an outline of crowd categories established, the May 4 shootings can be better defined from a social contagion perspective.

What Happened

On Monday, during a two-hour period (10:45 a.m.-12:45 p.m.), the crowd on the Commons participated in the basic forms of collective behavior. From milling, to collective behavior, to social contagion, the crowd perpetuated the elementary collective mechanisms.

In discussing the events of May 4, it is important to understand the events that led to Monday's explosive confrontation. On Thursday, April 30, President Nixon sent U.S. troops into Cambodia without the consent of Congress. At noon on Friday (May 1), a group of students buried a copy of the U.S. Constitution. Steve Sharoff, a graduate teaching assistant, led the rally. The group contended the Constitution had been murdered as Nixon didn't have the consent of Congress. Another rally was announced for noon on Monday. That night, students rioted in the downtown bar area of Kent and were eventually marched back to campus by city policy.

On Saturday (May 2), a large group of students gathered for an early evening rally on the Commons. They eventually burned down the ROTC building. When firemen came to distinguish the flames, they were pelted with rocks and their fire hoses were slashed. The Ohio National Guard was called in and, after clearing the Commons, maintained control of the campus. The Guard was called to Kent after spending four days monitoring a truckers' strike in Akron.

On Sunday (May 3), a festive mood prevailed as students returned to campus. The day passed without serious incident until a campus curfew was enforced on Sunday night. After numerous confrontations, the good feeling between the Guard and students clearly went up in smoke (tear gas). It should be pointed out that throughout the weekend KSU President Robert White was away from campus. Major decisions concerning the campus were made by the city and Governor Jim Rhodes (through the National Guard). The university had little say in the decision-making process as, with the President gone and the Provost ill, the chain of command led to four university vice-presidents. With this unstable situation, serving as a backdrop, Kent State stumbled onto an occurrence that shook the nation.

Classes were held as usual on Monday (May 4). It was a primary goal of Governor Rhodes that the university remain open. At the base of Monday's confusion was the injunction that prohibited assembly, peaceful or otherwise. Many students and faculty questioned the injunction as they believed the classroom to be an assembly of sorts. This was just one area where many students, faculty, and administrators were unsure of what was right or wrong.

At eleven o'clock on Monday morning, students were "milling" about on the Commons. The 9:55-10:45 classes had just ended and students were on their way to or from class; or merely enjoying the warm spring day. Many were aware of the noon rally that was scheduled, but due to ineffective communication, were not aware that it was "forbidden." "All outdoor demonstrations and gatherings are banned by order of the Governor" was announced over the school intercom and WKSU. Since the school intercom operated in only some of the classrooms (and none of the dorms) and WKSU was one of many radio stations, the banning of the noon rally was just another rumor.

As the eleven o'clock classes let out, the Commons became flooded with students. At 11:45, General Canterbury (commander of the Guard) became alarmed and ordered that the students disperse. At 11:48, someone began ringing the Victory Bell on the Commons (where the constitution had been buried on Friday). The riot act was read at various points on the Commons. A confused atmosphere was created. The milling intensified. Those on the Commons, regardless of their reason for being there, became sensitive to each other. All kinds of students (with diverse backgrounds) were drawn together and stimulated each other as they rallied behind a common question. "We've done nothing wrong. Why are we being dispersed?" The dispersal order was given long before any rocks had been thrown.

"Collective behavior" was then set in motion. Certain individuals standing by the Victory Bell worked to incite the crowd to action. At first the calls to action were only verbally approved by the crowd. But as the Guard began marching from the ROTC building through the Commons, firing tear gas, the calls to action were followed by irrational acts . . . from both sides.

Photographs during this time period show a broad spectrum of students on the Commons. As previously mentioned, only some of the students had come to the Commons for the rally. It was noon on a warm spring day. Whether they were on their way to or from class, throwing a frisbee, eating lunch, or merely enjoying the weather, the students on the Commons were legal in being there. Knowing this, the students became outraged when ordered to disperse. (It should be noted that a university vice-president was responsible for incorrectly announcing the prohibition of assembly, not the Guard. The Guard was following what they believed to be legal guidelines.) Regardless of their politics, the majority of students got swept into the final state of activity.

The "social contagion" base was laid when the Guard fired tear gas and approached the students. As if it were a rallying cry, students took turns taunting the Guard by running up and ringing the Victory Bell. As the Guard got closer an irrational appeal swept through the crowd. Rumors spread fast. Spectators became participants. Actions were dictated by group impulse. The line was clearly drawn between the Guard and students. Tear gas canisters were thrown back at the Guard along with rocks and obscenities. More confusion found its way onto the Commons as more students came across the area.

As the Guard came closer to Taylor Hall, their tear gas was inhaled into the building's air-conditioning system, affecting all those inside. Any inhabitants that would've evacuated from the front entrance (at the time of the shootings) would've been mowed down by the line of fire. With all the excitement on campus, many professors cancelled classes, encouraging students to observe the drama. All the while, the Guard and protestors were exchanging tear gas, rocks, and emotions.

When the Guard reached the practice football field, at the opposite end of the Commons from the ROTC building, sixteen enlisted men knelt on one knee and assumed firing position. Even as the Guardsmen aimed their rifles directly at the violent protestors, the taunting continued. After roughly twenty minutes, the Guard regrouped and backtracked towards the ROTC building. Many of the students were exuberant as they interpreted the move as a retreat.

Again, it must be stressed that, as each minute the confrontation unfolded, more and more students continued to pour onto the Commons area. Even though many of those new arrivals were only spectators, they added to the general confusion and explosive atmosphere.

The climax of the May 4 social contagion occurred when the Guard reached the top of Blanket Hill, midway back to the ROTC building. At that point, the Guard turned and fired into a crowd of students. In evaluating this incident from a social contagion perspective, it isn't so important that some uninvolved students were shot, as it is that the climate perpetuated the Guard (for whatever reason) to open fire in an indiscriminate manner.

The shootings created a numbing effect. Word spread quickly that they weren't firing blanks. The guns were loaded. Four people were dead, many were wounded. This was unbelievable and totally unacceptable.

From that cruel reality the social contagion became even more intense. The social contagion intensified as unarmed students gathered to charge on the armed Guardsmen. "Let them splatter us if they want to" and "let's finish it here and now" were the primary cries. General Canterbury issued an order stating that, unless the students dispersed from the area, there would be another confrontation. Fortunately, more rational minds were present and worked to avoid further violence. The university was closed. The dead and wounded were removed. The Commons was eventually cleared. All that remained were immediate memories.

The impact of the shootings was felt across the country as American education experienced it's first national student strike. Since then, many essays have been written about the collective behavior exhibited at Kent State during those four days in May. Most of the work has been of a nonacademic nature and there has been little systematic behavioral analysis done. The following theoretical application conveys an interpretation of a large body of data from a collective behavior episode.

Analysis of the Kent State Incident
Using Smelser's Theory of Collective Behavior

According to the theoretical model of collective behavior developed by Neil J. Smelser there are five determinants of collective behavior. Structural conduciveness, which suggests that social conditions are permissive for an occurrence of hostile outburst; structural strain, which describes conditions of strain that fall within conditions of conduciveness; growth of a generalized hostile belief, when beliefs prepare participants for the ensuing actions; mobilization of participants for action, which is the final stage of the value-added process that results in a hostile outburst; and control of hostile outbursts, which serves as a counterdeterminant.

Using the Smelser application, Jerry M. Lewis recognizes three categories of students as being on the Commons. The active core, the cheerleaders, and the spectators. The active core carried out the action toward the Guard by gestures, yells, and throwing rocks. The cheerleaders were those students who yelled in support of the core and against the Guard. The spectators simply observed what was going on.

Lewis goes on to apply the Smelser theory by acknowledging factors which comprise each of the previously mentioned five determinants. Under structural conduciveness, focus is centered on the structure of responsibility (of the Guard, students, and administration), the absence of communication channels, and communication among the aggrieved. With the structural strain, attention is placed primarily on the strain in norms and values (that students were used to peacefully congregating on the Commons).

In the growth and spread of a generalized belief, emphasis is placed on ambiguity (confusion), anxiety (over the "trespassing" Guard), and two precipitating factors (the well-publicized Monday rally and the Guard making a stand in front of the ROTC building). Mobilization for action is based on leadership (formal organization) and organization of the hostile outburst (preexisting crowd structure, ecological factors, and social control agencies). Regarding the control of hostile outbursts, Lewis summarizes that the Guard ineffectively applied force leading to the shootings. Rather than serving as a counterdeterminant, they acted as a precipitating factor in keeping the hostility level equal to, and higher than, before the outburst began.

Conclusion

Regarding Smelser's theory, when applied to the Kent State episode, I recognize its primary value in effectively interpreting the large amount of data. At the same time, due to its generalized base, I have doubts about its predictive application. Although I know of no study that deals with the Kent State shootings more specifically in this manner, I think the Lewis application of Smelser's theory would be enhanced greatly if he could narrow his focus in a more detailed manner.

"The Guard"

One aspect of the Kent State episode that detracts considerably from any analysis is the absence of information concerning the National Guard. With the information known by the public, we can only construct a vague outline of the Guard perspective. Beyond that, analysis is merely speculative.

In literature dealing with the shootings there is considerable analysis of the student perspective and the various types of students involved. But with the Guardsmen, not much is said about the individuals that comprised the Guard. Throughout my research, "the Guard" conjures thoughts of some strange hybrid between a right-wing conservative and a robot (geared towards "law and order"). Not much is mentioned about the fatigue the Guardsmen were experiencing as they arrived in Kent after being on call for four days during a truckers strike in Akron. Not much is said about the individual personalities that were carrying those loaded M-1 rifles. We know a lot about the individual students involved and their collective action. But we know very little about the individuals that comprised "the Guard."

Minutes after the shootings a veil of silence fell between the Guard and the public. There's been minimal accounting of the individuals and motivating factors behind their actions. Until this veil is lifted, allowing us to learn more about the men of "the Guard," we can only be content with half of this complex story.

Notes

Adamek, R.J. and Lewis, J.M. "Social Control Violence and Radicalization: The Kent State Case," *Social Forces*, March 1973, 342-347.

Davies, P. *The Truth About Kent State: A Challenge to the American Conscience*. New York: Farrar, Straus & Giroux, 1973.

Eszterhas, J. *Thirteen Seconds: Confrontation at Kent State*. New York: Dodd, Mead, 1970.

Furlong, W.B. "The Guardsmen's View of the Tragedy at Kent State," *The New York Times Magazine*, June 21, 1970, 12-13, 64, 68-69, 71.

Hughes, H. *Crowd and Mass Behavior*. Boston: Allyn and Bacon, 1972.

LeBon, G. *The Crowd*. New York: Viking Press, 1972.

Lewis, J.M. "Review Essay: The Telling of Kent State," *Social Problems*, Fall, 1971, 267-279.

Lewis, J.M. "A Study of the Kent State Incident Using Smelser's Theory of Collective Behavior," *Sociological Inquiry*, No. 2, 1972, 87-96.

Meier, A. and Rudwick, E. "The Kent State Affair: Social Control of a Putative-Value Oriented Movement," *Sociological Inquiry*, No. 2, 1972, 81-86.

Michener, J. *Kent State: What Happened and Why*. New York: Random House, 1971.

O'Neil, R.M. *No Heroes, No Villians*. San Francisco: Jossey-Bass, 1972.

Park, R. *The Crowd and the Public*. Chicago: The University of Chicago Press, 1972.

Sale, K. *SDS*. New York: Vintage Books, 1973.

Special Report: The U.S. President's Commission on Campus Unrest. New York: Arno Press, 1970.

Stone, I.F. *The Killings at Kent State: How Murder Went Unpunished*. New York: Vintage Books, 1971.

Thompkins, P. and Anderson, E.V. *Communication Crisis at Kent State*. Columbus, OH: Ohio State University Press, 1971.

"Violence and Understanding: Campus Unrest and the Scranton Report," *Catholic World*, December, 1970, 119-122.

Warren, W. *The Middle of the Country: The Events of May 4th*. New York: Avon, 1970.

Chapter Five

Organizational Culture and Conflict Resolution: A Study of a Greek Lettered Social Organization

Author's Note: The organization analyzed in this study exhibited behavior that was sexist and crude. My intention in writing this chapter is to report the activities I observed in a social science framework (not to make judgments or offer suggestions for improvement).

In recent years, the concept of organizational culture has received increased attention as a viable perspective from which organizations can be studied. This has been evidenced in a variety of publications (Deal and Kennedy, 1982; Pacanowsky and Putnam, 1983; Schwartz and Davis, 1981; Pacanowsky and O'Donnel-Trujillo, 1983; Carbaugh, 1985a). The purpose of this chapter is to analyze the relationship of organizational culture and organizational conflict resolution communication as evidenced through behaviors of organization members. A collegiate greek lettered social organization was selected for study due to the strong identity such organizations promote. Collegiate greek lettered social organizations are acknowledged as a distinct type of organization on college campuses (Amiot and Cottingham, 1976; Barth, 1964; Leemon, 1972).

Organizational culture is defined as "the spoken system of symbols, symbolic forms, and meanings that constitute and enacts a common sense of work-life" (Carbaugh, 1985b). Similar definitions and paralleled applications are provided by a variety of theorists (Harris, 1985; Pacanowsky and O'Donnel-Trujillo, 1982). Furthermore, "the cultural analyst's immediate chore is to discover and interpret the spoken systems that are used in organizations' particular socio-cultural context" (Carbaugh, 1985b).

Deal and Kennedy (1982, 13-15) describe five specific elements that can be analyzed to understand the culture of an organization: environment, values, heroes, rites and rituals, and the cultural network. The environment, whether it is a business or social environment, is shaped by the goals and objectives of the organization. Values are the basic concepts and beliefs of the organization and they serve to define "success" in concrete terms for members. Heroes personify the values of the culture and act as role models for others. Rites and rituals are systematic and programmed routines of day-to-day life in the organization. The formal rites and rituals provide visible examples of what the organization stands for. The cultural network ties everything together by serving as a carrier of values and mythology and providing an informal network for the hidden hierarchy of power. These five elements are the basis for any culture (Harris, 1985).

The study of organizational cultures is useful, in not only clarifying those elements which mold the organization, but in providing direction for development within the organization. Such application is exemplified in "Using Interpretive Research: The Development of a Socialization Program at RCA." In this study, Gary Kreps describes how an organizational socialization program was developed based on the existing organizational culture of the primary organization (Kreps, 1983).

I have used pseudonyms in the place of real names of those individuals and organizations discussed in this study. It is my intention that these individuals and organizations not be adversely affected by my analysis.

The Beta chapter of Sigma Tau Omega was established at Midwestern State University in 1862. Since that time, Beta chapter has never closed its doors, making it the oldest continuously active chapter within Sigma Tau Omega Fraternity. There are 120 chapters that maintain active and alumni membership of over 100,000 Sig Taus. *The Good Sig Tau*, a pamphlet distributed to each member of the fraternity, outlines the basic principles of Sigma Tau Omega. The fraternity concept is based on close brotherhood, secrecy and initiation, patriotism and civic-mindedness, and student control of fraternity life. Emphasis is stressed on a "triple-headed strategy for brotherhood": social improvement, moral improvement, and intellectual improvement. A portion of the Sig Tau creed exemplifies the aforementioned.

I believe in Sigma Tau Omega as an abiding influence to help me do my work, fulfill my obligations, maintain my self-respect, and bring about that happy life wherein I may more truly love my fellow man, serve my country, and obey my God. (*The Good Sig Tau*, 1977, 3)

The Beta chapter, during the period of the study, had roughly forty active members who lived in the Sig Tau House during the academic school year. Members were from predominantly middle-class/upper-class backgrounds. The fraternity membership managed the chapter within fundamental guidelines established by the Sigma Tau Omega national office in Indianapolis, Indiana. General membership meetings were held once a week. These meetings, as well as other fraternity business, were governed by fraternity officers.

Prospective members were selected and initiated through a pledge program. A pledge program was formulated three times a year as a means of training prospective members for possible admission to the fraternity. A pledge class was started at the beginning of the fall, winter, and spring quarters. The pledge period lasted ten weeks and was intended to orient the prospective member (pledge) to fraternity life and initiate him into the organization.

Field research methods were used to gather data during the period of the study. I had one extensive period of contact with the fraternity beginning March, 1980 and ending August, 1983. During this period, I was employed as the Proctor (head resident) of the Sig Tau chapter. In this capacity, I supervised the overall running of the House and served as a contact person when outside agencies (i.e., university Greek life coordinator, city police, neighboring fraternities, etc.) contacted the fraternity. I lived in the fraternity house throughout the study. My involvement with the fraternity included chapter meetings, individual committee meetings, meals, social events, informal recreation, drinking beer with members in the uptown bar district, and other day-to-day aspects of fraternity life.

In "Naturalistic Research Traditions," Charles Bantz (1983, 55-71) describes six naturalistic research methods: participant observation, interviews, organizational documents, training/instructional manuals, organizational outputs, and memoirs. Each of these methods were utilized to gather data.

Throughout the field study, I maintained comprehensive notes based on participant observation encounters. Informative interviews were conducted with twelve primary interviewees of Sigma Tau Omega. Their positions within the fraternity ranged from fraternity president to pledge. Organizational documents studied included the Sigma Tau Omega Chapter Management Guide and *Spectrum* (a monthly publication of the Sigma Tau Omega National Office). The primary training/instructional manual is *The Good Sig Tau*, which is used as the pledge education manual for prospective fraternity members. Organizational outputs include articles, letters to the editor, and advertisements published in the university student newspaper. Literature studied, which was written by and about the fraternity, is listed in appendix A.

Two memoirs, one by an active member and one by a Sig Tau alumnus (Heminger, 1975), were also reviewed. The aforementioned active member, Alan Neff, was an English major who kept a diary that detailed his life in the fraternity. Upon graduation, he allowed me to read through his diary. This was beneficial as I could compare my observations of events with his observations of the same events.

In addition, I administered a one-page survey to the fraternity membership near the end of the study. Survey questions were based on findings realized from participant observation encounters and interviews. The survey is located in appendix B.

As stated in the introduction, the purpose of this chapter is to analyze the relationship of organizational culture and organizational conflict resolution communication. I will define the organizational culture of Sigma Tau Omega by describing the organizational culture elements set forth by Deal and Kennedy (1982, 13-15), as evidenced within Sigma Tau Omega. The described culture of Sigma Tau Omega will then be used as a perspective from which the conflict resolution communication can be interpreted.

The Organizational Culture of Sigma Tau Omega

The organizational culture elements, as evidenced within Sigma Tau Omega, will be described through phenomena that are representative of each element.

Environment. The environment is shaped by the goals and objectives of the organization. As a social fraternity, the environment of Sigma Tau Omega is best described through their parties, pranks, and the threat of physical violence.

The Sig Taus had at least one party each week during the period of the study. These parties ranged from "Teas" (parties with sororities), porch parties, room parties, and special occasion parties. Beer was always available at Sig Tau parties. It seemed as if there was a party for any occasion imaginable.

The Mental Ward parties were a consistent favorite among the membership. These parties featured roughly fifty kegs of beer and were open to the public. The principle idea being that those in attendance could get thoroughly inebriated on beer and other social intoxicants and "go crazy." Porch parties and room parties occurred on many Thursdays, Fridays, and Saturdays when other parties were not planned.

Life at the Sig Tau House consisted of pranks directed toward specific members, the fraternity in general, and the local community. Fraternity members were tolerant of the antics perpetuated by fellow members. Most pranks were committed against specific members. Dana Keller, who was legally blind, frequently had his room rearranged when he was gone from the House. One winter morning the members built a wall of snow covering the front door so they could watch him walk into it. Dana later told me "it comes with the turf."

Random pranks directed toward the general membership occurred less frequently. Such pranks ranged from tearing the House phone out of the wall to putting additives in the food. One night after we had brownies for dessert, we realized someone had added a social intoxicant to the recipe.

Pranks against the local community generally occurred during the spring. A typical prank involved firing flaming tennis balls from a long metal tube doused on the inside with lighter fluid. This was done at night from the House roof, and when pedestrians were within "scaring range" balls would be fired toward the sidewalk and fraternity members would yell "incoming!" at people on the sidewalk, as if the pedestrians were engaged in some type of warfare.

The threat of physical violence was a backdrop for interactions within the House. A typical physical confrontation is exemplified through an interaction between Carmen Merinelli and Wally Butler. After a late night party at the House, Carmen walked through the hallways and sprayed members at random with a fire extinguisher. Carmen sprayed Wally in the face and Wally called

Carmen a vulgar term. Carmen put down the extinguisher, pointed to his own chin, and said "C'mon, I dare you." Wally got two good punches to Carmen's face before other members split them apart. Ned Wagner (President) later told me: "Man, it's winter and everybody just gets uptight and tired . . . we need to blow off steam . . . just so nobody gets hurt." Wally, in explaining his feelings about the fight said, "I hate a lot of these idiots anyway . . . I could probably work on liking them, but why should I, when I hate 'em . . . it's stupid cause we're supposed to be brothers."

More often than not, members would apologize to each other within a few days of a physical fight, especially if they were drinking beer previous to the fight. I rarely witnessed genuine hate during confrontations such as physical fights. An unspoken rule seemed to be "just so nobody gets hurt."

Values. Values "define 'success' in concrete terms for members—'if you do this, you too will be a success'—and establish standards of achievement within the organization" (Deal and Kennedy, 1982, 13-14). The values within Sigma Tau Omega were evidenced through views on money, recognition, and how they, as an organization, viewed women.

The Sig Taus did not discuss their personal financial situations very often. Most discussions about financial matters dealt with how much they would make in their intended occupations. I met no Sig Tau who was not at least partially subsidized by his parents. Members were rarely ostentatious with their material possessions, although my experience with alumni indicated a stronger concern in showing their wealth.

The fraternity promoted different types of recognition. Types of recognition included the Top Twenty Award, given by the national organization to the twenty top ranked chapters in the country; formal recognition at chapter meetings and outside meetings; and the "Dink of the Week," which was awarded to the member who committed the gravest social error.

Formal recognition of members was acknowledged at chapter meetings and in Sig Tau publications. Each year Service Awards were voted upon and presented at chapter meetings. Service Awards were presented to the freshman, sophomore, junior, and senior who made the biggest contributions to the fraternity. Distinguished alumni were frequently acknowledged in Sig Tau publications.

Informal recognition was frequently given in and outside of meetings. The following situation exemplifies such recognition. "Brad Yarnell, alumni relations officer, thanked three members who helped with the homecoming dinner last night. The membership applauded after thanks was given." The aforementioned occurred during a chapter meeting. The Dink of the Week was awarded each week at chapter meetings. The Dink of the Week trophy was presented to the member who committed the gravest social error during the previous week. It was first awarded to Skip Hansen, the day after he vomited in his dates' purse.

Being a social fraternity, the membership placed a high priority on their interactions with women. I know of no member who did not have at least one date during the period of the study. Each spring the fraternity elected a "sweetheart" to represent the Sig Taus at various Sig Tau functions throughout the following academic year. A picture of the sweetheart was hung in the television room. The sweetheart was always dating a member of the fraternity at the time of her election to the position. The membership was generally respectful of the sweetheart and their own steady girlfriends. However, relations with other women were frequently abusive and the subject of much conversation among the members.

Heroes. Heroes "personify the values of the culture and act as role models" (Harris, 1985, 7). Jack Armstrong best exemplified this position among the membership. He served as chapter president during the first year of the study. He was an autocratic leader and frequently dealt with problems in a direct manner. Jack was a boxer on the Midwestern State University boxing team and he made it clear he would use force to enforce fraternity rules.

Don Ingram, nicknamed Jed because of his "wild" tendencies, broke the kitchen door by slamming it "for kicks." At the next chapter meeting Jack Armstrong stated his feelings about the broken door during the President's Report. Jack: "I wanna know who broke the door and I wanna know now. . . . Some of you guys know who did it, but I wanna give the guilty person a chance to be a man about it." There was a thirty-second pause as Jack stared at various faces in the room. Jed: "Thank me. I did it." This was a typical approach for Jack to use.

Comments about Jack during interviews served to elaborate on this observation. Norm Egan: "He was an authoritarian . . . but he was fair. Even if he didn't like you, but you were a brother, he'd do his best to help you out . . . he'd punch if necessary." Rudy Shnider: "Armstrong was a legend in his own time . . . guys knew he'd punch. . . . His time in office was more like an era." Jim Hangen: "John (who followed Jack as President) is a shadow of Armstrong . . . but he's not nearly as strong." Jack believed in structure, authority, follow-through and "sticking by my guns, even when I mess up; in the long run guys will respect you for it."

Rites and Rituals. Rites and rituals are the systematic and programed routines of day-to-day life in an organization. They provide the potent and visible examples of what the organization stands for (Deal and Kennedy, 1982, 14-15). Rites and rituals within Sigma Tau Omega were best exemplified through formal rituals, the pledge program, and informal rituals.

Formal ritual was taken seriously by the chapter members. I heard some nasty jokes alleged against each other's girlfriends, but I never heard jokes about fraternity rituals.

The Ritual of our Fraternity is the one element of Sigma Tau Omega that you will share with all Sig Taus across the continent. It expresses the essence and purpose of the good Sig Tau. . . . We have seen our Fraternity grow, develop and change substantially, but our men have enjoyed the same sense of brotherhood down through our 120 years. This is why our Ritual means so much today; the Sig Tau initiated today relates to all other Sig Taus of his and other generations because both have reacted to an identical personal experience. (*The Good Sig Tau*, 1977, 9)

The formal ritual was established by the national office of the fraternity.

Sig Tau ritual was initially instilled in new members during the pledge program. The pledge program lasted for one academic quarter and ended in a final "hell" week. Aside from the formal ritual, there were many informal traditions the new pledge experienced. For example, during the pledge period, the pledges entered the House through the side door, referred to active members as sir/Mr., answered the House phone, and each time they used a set of steps they had to state the names of the eight founding fathers of Sigma Tau Omega. The House was designed with eight sets of steps, each set containing eight steps. During hell week, they slept in the basement, wore their "scummy clothes" (jeans and a t-shirt that were not washed all week) in the House, served meals to actives, and were generally harassed throughout each night, leaving little time for sleep.

There were a variety of informal traditional activities that occurred in recognition of events such as birthdays, pinnings (when a member gave his fraternity pin to his girlfriend to acknowledge preengagement), and engagements. On the day of a member's birthday, he was customarily carried out to the college green (area directly across the street from the House) after dinner, his clothes were removed from him, and the leftovers from dinner were poured on him. Then the member would be left to run back across the green to the House. This was called "greening." If a member got pinned, his head was dunked in the toilet and the toilet was flushed. This was called a "swirley."

When a member got engaged, he was carried to the house (usually a sorority house) where his girlfriend lived and chained to a tree (or similar stationary object). That is, he was stripped to his underwear and the chain was run through his underwear and locked to the tree. This left the member in an awkward position whereby he would lose his underwear if he ran away. A bucket of dinner leftovers was then poured on him. By this time, there generally would be numerous spectators and the member's girlfriend would be allowed to offer the member a towel to cover himself with.

The following question was asked on the fraternity survey. "In what way is tradition important within the fraternity? Why?" Eighty percent of those surveyed strongly advocated the need for tradition. The need for tradition was related with the importance of brotherhood and consistency among actives and alumni. As stated by Rudy Shnider, a recipient of all three of the aforementioned informal rituals, "Tradition is what this place is based on. . . . I really like the idea of knowing I can come back in twenty years and have a place to come to."

Cultural Network. The cultural network is an informal means of communication that serves as a backdrop for life in the organization. It communicates values and it carries the hidden hierarchy of power within the organization (Deal and Kennedy, 1982, 15). The cultural network in Sigma Tau Omega was evidenced through clothing, language, the role of professional football, and the different academic majors.

Clothing styles at the Sig Tau House were consistently conservative. Practically all members owned jackets which had "The Sig Taus" written on the back.

The Sigma Tau Omega greek letters were frequently inscribed on shirts, hats, shorts, sweatpants, and sweatshirts. "Preppy" clothes were also popular. Typical preppy clothes included "topsiders" worn without socks (brown deck shoes), clean jeans, Izod sport shirt with an alligator on the left breast and, in cooler weather, a long sleeve dress shirt over the sport shirt. Periodically, a fad would occur, and a group of Sig Taus would follow it. Such fads included cutting the sleeves off of long-sleeved hooded sweaters, wearing black rimmed sunglasses, and carrying a bandanna in one's back pocket.

Language deviation was abundantly clear through fraternity jargon. Practically all jargon had sexual overtones. It is not suitable for inclusion in this chapter due to the vulgar nature of the jargon.

Members frequently argued about pro football teams during the football season. Heated arguments occurred at times and, if both parties were stubborn about their beliefs, a bet would be made regarding speculation of the season's outcome. When rival teams played on television, group members would generally align with either team. It became my opinion members used the pro football teams as a means to express like or dislike for other members. That is, if a disliked member's favorite team was losing a game, certain members might exhibit exaggerated enthusiasm because the team was losing.

The following question was asked on the fraternity survey. "It is common for fraternity members to root against a pro football team. In such situations, do you think fraternity members are rooting against the pro football team or against other members who happen to be strong fans of the pro football team?" Fifty three percent of the respondents indicated members were rooting against other members, 11 percent of the respondents indicated members were rooting against the pro football team, and 28 percent of the respondents indicated members were rooting against both members and the pro football team. Thus, members could express dislike for each other without overtly stating the dislike (i.e., "the Cleveland Browns are worthless" could carry the same context as "you're worthless").

Similarly, members periodically assailed the academic major being studied by another member with the same underlying effect (i.e., if a management major was mad at an organizational communication major he might say "organizational communication is for idiots who can't pass the management math requirement"). Thus, a base was laid for members to covertly express dislike for each other without overtly acknowledging personal dislikes.

Conflict Resolution Communication within Sigma Tau Omega Fraternity

A primary objective of this study is to better understand the organizational conflict resolution communication within Sigma Tau Omega by considering the role of organizational culture in providing a backdrop for such occurrences. The following discussion explains approaches used in conflict resolution communication, describes the variety of issues encountered, correlates these approaches with conflict resolution communication theory, and clarifies how these approaches worked. Throughout this discussion, the role of previously described organizational culture elements will be evidenced.

The fraternity used voting in formal settings and, at times, resolved issues through discussion. Voting was the established procedure for conflict resolution and decision making. The informal hierarchy was based on fraternity office held (if any), physical size, wit, and pin number (seniority). Participation within the organization led to knowledge about the functioning of the organization, which in turn led to referent power within the organization. Such participation was usually acknowledged when involved members were elected to fraternity offices.

Formal Conflict Resolution. The fraternity held chapter meetings each Sunday night throughout the academic year. Attendance was mandatory and meetings usually lasted about an hour. The President presided over the chapter meetings and utilized a formal agenda. Inputs and comments were directed to the President. He was responsible for running meetings in accordance with the fraternity constitution. Each President, during the period of the study, evidenced his knowledge of the Sig Tau constitution and the enforcement of these regulations.

Voting was the main method of decision making and conflict resolution. The chapter would usually discuss an issue until it was approved or disapproved. A ballot or verbal vote was taken if there was disagreement. Casual votes were frequently taken on less controversial issues; the President would ask for a show of hands, but not bother to count if a majority was evident. Exceptions to the use of voting occurred when the Executive Board or individual officers, such as the President, could make decisions without a chapter vote. Such exceptions were designated within the constitution and bylaws.

Informal Conflict Resolution. An informal hierarchy existed within the Sig Tau House. The hierarchy was based on the office held within the fraternity (if any), physical size of the member, wit of the member, and the member's pin number (seniority). The President was at the top of the office hierarchy. Chapter President was a formal position, but its power carried over into informal conflict resolution situations. The President not only held a position that evidenced the respect the membership had for him, he also gained a powerful position regarding the enforcement of bylaws. Other offices included vice-president, treasurer, secretary, pledge master (in charge of the pledge program), and the house manager (in charge of physical maintenance).

Physical size, and its correlation with being a good fighter, carried influence in the informal hierarchy. Once a member established himself as a good fighter, his threat would be interpreted as the final warning before he would attack. Jack Armstrong showed himself to be a competent fighter during his freshman and sophomore years, but I never knew him to punch another member during his junior and senior years. He had a reputation for punching and the membership stopped cold in their tracks on the occasions he made threats.

A good wit could aid a member's informal influence. Everybody in the House was vulnerable to the wit of fellow members. Such vulnerable areas included the attractiveness of one's girlfriend, one's academic major, one's grade point average, and one's physical appearance. These types of verbal jabs were frequently shared at the Sig Tau House. Receiving such comments generally served to indicate that one was accepted. Circumstances seemed to dictate the influence of wit in the House. Such circumstances included who was present, the setting, who made the statement, and who (if anybody) was the butt of the joke.

Pin numbers were assigned to members when they pledged the fraternity. Thus, older members had lower pin numbers and newer members had higher pin numbers. The lower the pin number the higher the seniority. Pin numbers were used in the room selection process and for deciding which members would be given the four parking spaces in the House driveway. Pin numbers also offered an abstract referent power. That is, members who had been affiliated with the chapter for a long time who had lower pin numbers were periodically referred to for advice on how things were done or "how things used to be."

The following question was asked in the fraternity survey: "In informal situations (outside of meetings), which one of the following factors most strongly affects an individual's influence?" Many members indicated more than one factor. The following percentages reflect how many times each factor was indicated by the respondents.

42%   office held in the fraternity

42%   physical size of the member

24%   pin number

39%   wit, sense of humor, etc.

Ninety-seven separate issues were analyzed during the period of the study. These issues were selected for analysis as they were representative of behavior and phenomena consistently recognized during the period of the study. Each of these typical issues were classified according to the setting they occurred in, formal or informal, and the level of controversy which occurred, high or low level. Thus, there are four quadrants: high-level controversy issues in formal settings, low-level controversy issues in formal settings, high-level controversy issues in informal settings, and low-level controversy issues in informal settings.

Formal settings were limited to chapter meetings and individual committee meetings. Informal settings included all other situations. The distinction between high- and low-level controversy issues was more arbitrary. I viewed all issues as being on one continuum, regarding controversy, and worked to recognize them for the degree of controversy they represented within the fraternity. Thus, issues representing a higher degree of controversy were classified as high-level controversy issues and issues representing a lower degree of controversy were classified as low-level controversy issues.

Aside from the setting and degree of controversy, distinctions were also recognized according to the types of issues. Table 1 outlines four types of issues: logistics, finances, principle, and personality. Issues of logistics involved the physical maintenance and day-to-day management of the fraternity. Issues of finance involved organizational expenses and the distribution of funds. Issues of principle involved ethical questions and the interpretation of the fraternity's philosophical base. Issues of personality involved differences between members.

Table 1
Four Quadrants of Conflict Resolution Attempts

	Formal Settings	Informal Settings
High-Level Controversy	Issues of Logistics: 7 Issues of Finance: 6 Issues of Principle: 1	Issues of Logistics: 4 Issues of Finance: 6 Issues of Personality: 13
Low-Level Controversy	Issues of Logistics: 19 Issues of Finance: 3 Issues of Personality: 7	Issues of Logistics: 6 Issues of Finance: 6 Issues of Principle: 2 Issues of Personality: 17

Conflict is expressed through communication. The communication, if it's verbal, nonverbal, or written, serves to convey meaning. Throughout the field study, I not only observed conflict resolution, I more specifically made observations of the communication that the conflict was expressed through. As such, communication was the expressive mode that served as the conduit for conflict between (or among) the involved parties. Over time, patterns occurred that grew into trends.

Pondy (1967, 296-320) synthesizes conflict concepts and models and defines conflict through a sequence of five events; latent conflict, perceived conflict, felt conflict, manifest conflict, and conflict aftermath. This sequence was more evident with high-level controversy issues, rather than low-level controversy issues, as high-level controversy issues were more intense and feelings were more explicitly expressed. One could more readily recognize high-level controversy issues progressing from latent conflict and perceived conflict through felt conflict, manifest conflict, and conflict aftermath by observing the communication expressed among involved members. Low-level controversy issues evidenced the same sequence, but in a less obvious manner due to the intensity of the issues.

Robbins explains that conflict has a number of causes and can be separated into three categories: communication, structure, and personal-behavior factors. Conflict evolving from the communicative source represents problems related with semantic difficulties, misunderstandings, and noise in communication channels. Structural conflict deals with organizational roles and barriers that are often introduced by management. Personal-behavior factors are based on personal value systems (Robbins, 1974, 29-30). Most of the issues I observed in the four quadrants of conflict resolution, involved personal-behavior factors. Although there were issues involving the communicative sources and structural factors, most conflicts in Sigma Tau Omega stemmed from personal-behavior factors.

"Conflict between parties that mutually perceive themselves to be equal in power and legitimacy is more difficult to resolve cooperatively than when there is a mutual recognition of differential power and legitimacy" (Deutsch, 1973, 44). This proposition was evidenced in my analysis of the fraternity conflict resolution communication. The fraternity overtly acknowledged differential power and legitimacy among its members; this usually aided effective conflict resolution.

A primary finding in this study deals with how those who exhibit power in conflict resolution communication situations are able to attain and maintain such a position. The data indicates participation within the organization led to knowledge about the functioning of the organization, which in turn led to referent power within the organization. Such participation was usually acknowledged when involved members were voted into fraternity offices.

There were four presidents during the period of the study and all four served in subordinate offices before becoming president. A common progression was for the freshman and sophomore members to fulfill subordinate offices and functions within the fraternity, and juniors and seniors generally filled the highest offices. That is, the executive officers had always *participated* at lower levels, attained *knowledge* about the organization and its processes, and worked into positions of higher *power*.

In reflecting on the ramifications of the participation-knowledge-referent power progression, I have sought to understand if this progression is common in other types of organizations and if this progression is attributable to the particular organizational culture. An example of an exception is evidenced in the U.S. military. In the Air Force, for example, Chief Master Sergeants (enlisted rank) are commonly recognized for their referent power over junior grade officers. Although any junior grade officer (Second Lieutenant through Captain) formally outranks a Chief Master Sergeant, the junior grade officer will frequently rely on senior grade enlisted personnel for their referent power. Such a contradiction between the informal and formal chains of command is clearly attributable to the organizational culture as the formal ranking structure is established through Air Force regulation.

My findings in this study indicate a direct connection between organizational culture and conflict resolution communication approaches within the organization. A question for further study is "could better approaches to conflict resolution communication be developed by altering the culture of an organization?" This study is offered as a base for such analysis.

Notes

Amiot, W.K. and Cottingham, E.M. *Brotherhood: Myth or Mystique?* Indianapolis, IN: Sigma Nu, Inc., 1976.

Bantz, C. "Naturalistic Research Traditions," in M. Pacanowsky and L.L. Putnam, *Communication and Organizations: An Interpretive Approach.* Beverly Hills: Sage Publications, 1983.

Barth, R.E. *A Study of the Values of Fraternity Men and Non-Fraternity Men.* Unpublished M.A. Thesis, Ohio University, 1964.

Carbaugh, D. "Cultural Communication and Organizing," *International and Intercultural Communication Annual,* 9, 1985a, chapter 2.

Carbaugh, D. "Cultural Communication as Organization: A Case Study of Speech in an Organizational Setting." Paper presented at the annual meeting of the Speech Communication Association, Denver, CO, 1985b.

Deal, T.E. and Kennedy, A.A. *Corporate Culture: The Rites and Rituals of Corporate Life.* Reading, MA: Addison-Wesley, 1982.

Deutsch, M. *The Resolution of Conflict: Constructive and Destructive Process.* New Haven, CT: Yale University Press, 1973.

Harris, T. "Characteristics of Organizational Cultures: A Communication Perspective." Paper presented at the annual meeting of the Speech Communication Association, Denver, CO, 1985.

Heminger, E.L. *Sigma Tau Omega: A Reflection of Society.* Princeton, NJ: Princeton University Press, 1975.

Kreps, G.L. "Using Interpretive Research: The Development of a Socialization Program at RCA," in M. Pacanowsky and L.L. Putnam, *Communication and Organizations: An Interpretive Approach.* Beverly Hills: Sage Publications, 1983.

Leemon, T.A. *The Rites of Passage in a Student Culture.* New York: Columbia University Press, 1972.

Pacanowsky, M. and N. O'Donnel-Trujillo. "Communication and Organizational Cultures," *Western Journal of Speech,* 46 (1982).

Pacanowsky, M. and N. O'Donnel-Trujillo. "Organizational Communication as Cultural Performance," *Communication Monographs,* 50 (1983).

Pacanowsky, M. and Putnam, L.L.. *Communication and Organizations: An Interpretive Approach.* Beverly Hills: Sage Publications, 1983.

Pondy, L.R. "Organizational Conflict: Concepts and Models," *Administrative Science Quarterly,* 12 (1967).

Robbins, S.P. *Managing Organizational Conflict: A Nontraditional Approach.* Englewood Cliffs, NJ: Prentice-Hall, 1974.

Schwartz, H. and H. Davis. "Matching Corporate Culture and Business Strategy," *Organizational Dynamics*, Summer, 1981.

The Good Sig Tau. Indianapolis, IN: Sigma Tau Omega, 1977.

Appendix A

Fraternity Literature Reviewed

Advertisements for Sigma Tau Omega in the *Midwestern State University Post.*

Articles about the Sigma Tau Omega chapter in the *Midwestern State University Post.*

Beta Chapter of Sigma Tau Omega History handout. Obtained during Rush week. Fall, 1981.

The Good Sig Tau, a pledge education manual. Indianapolis, IN: Sigma Tau Omega, 1977.

Letters between the Sigma Tau Omega Director of Program Development and the Sigma Tau Omega Proctor at Midwestern State University.

Letters to the Editor, written by/about Sigma Tau Omega members, in the *Midwestern State University Post.*

Sigma Tau Omega Chapter Management Guide, 1934 (revised 1977).

Spectrum. A monthly publication of the Sigma Tau Omega National Office.

Appendix B

Fraternity Survey

How long have you been a fraternity member?

What was your motivation for joining the fraternity?

_____ social   _____ save money   _____ political

_____ other _____

Which of the following best describes your membership status?

_____ member
_____ committee chairman
_____ administrative council member

Which of the following best describes the economic background you grew up in?

_____ lower class
_____ lower-middle class
_____ middle class
_____ upper-middle class
_____ upper class

In what way is tradition important within the fraternity?

Why?

In informal conflict situations (outside of meetings), which one of the following factors most strongly affects an individual's influence:

_____ office held within the fraternity
_____ physical size of the member
_____ pin number
_____ wit, sense of humor, etc.
_____ other _____

If a fraternity member consistently violated the standards/philosophy of the fraternity and a majority of the membership wanted to cancel the individual's membership what would be a logical and fair approach in dealing with such a situation?

If a fellow fraternity member borrowed $50 from you to go on vacation, and then (after six months of avoiding you) made it clear he wasn't going to pay you back . . . would you most likely:

_____ take him to court
_____ verbally threaten the person
_____ physically threaten the person
_____ physically assault the person
_____ other _____

Do fraternity members who do a lot of extra work for the fraternity receive adequate recognition for their extra efforts? If so, what are some of the forms of such recognition?

If a member doesn't do his work duty, should he be allowed to eat dinner?

It is common for fraternity members to root against a pro football team. In such situations, do you think members are rooting against the pro football team or against other members who happen to be strong fans of the pro football team?

Chapter Six

The Intrapersonal Issue of Maintaining Researcher Detachment in Communication Ethnography

This chapter will deal with the intrapersonal issue of maintaining researcher detachment in communication ethnography. It will specifically focus on participant observation, an ethnographic research method, and the effect it can have on the self-concept of the participant observer. Participant observation allows for what Howard S. Becker explains as, "rich experiential context of observation of the event and observation of previous and following events" (Filstead, 1970, 141). Discussion of participant observation in relation to the intrapersonal issue of researcher detachment is relevant because much of the legitimacy of the participant observation method (and any method) rests on researcher objectivity.

Participant observation inquiry has been used to investigate a variety of research questions. In "A Naturalistic Study of the Meanings of Touch," Jones and Yarbrough (1985) used participant observation to examine the meanings-in-context of touching reported by persons from their daily interactions. Similarly, Owen (1984) used participant observation to study teacher classroom management communication. Gerry Philipsen used participant observation in "Speaking 'Like a Man' in Teamsterville" to find how groups view speaking as an effective means of social influence. Philipsen (1975, 22) states there is a lack of information in this area and this deficit "should be remedied by descriptive and comparative studies of American speech communities." The study described in this report is such a study.

The intrapersonal distinction the researcher stresses between depth of participation and degree of personal involvement is likely to affect his or her self-concept regarding where he or she stands in relation to the phenomenon being studied. I believe researchers who undertake participant observation studies are likely to experience an altered self-concept as a result of their field experience. The degree of alteration is related to the degree of personal involvement. The greater the personal involvement the greater the likelihood of an altered self-concept.

Researchers' discussions of personal impacts resulting from their inquiries is limited. Review of participant observation studies reveals a tendency of participant observers to describe specific procedures but to provide little discussion of personal experiences.

> Reports about field research usually describe the methods and techniques of the research. Less often do they tell of the researcher's social and emotional experience. . . . These topics are more often discussed in personal conversations between field researchers than written about in the literature. (Shaffir, Stebbins, and Turowetz, 1980, vii)

I have been surprised at the lack of discussion of personal experiences by participant observers. "What good is a research design that does not include some reference to those who will execute it" (Hughes, 1964, 82) or have executed it? Understanding of the message can be enhanced with an understanding of the messenger.

Researcher detachment from the phenomenon being studied regarding his or her personal orientation is largely an intrapersonal issue. That is, the distinction between his or her personal orientation and the phenomenon under study is constructed and maintained primarily through intrapersonal communication processes. Regardless of the degree of detachment maintained by the researcher, it is understandable the researcher will feel some degree of introspection during his or her study. My interest, regarding this introspection, is with personal effects felt by participant observers as a result of their research and the impact of such effects on researcher self-concept. This analysis will include a description of my experiences as a participant observer and the subsequent personal effects I have felt. I should reiterate my view that these personal effects are normal and acceptable as long as they do not interfere with data collection.

A dilemma inherent with participant observation occurs when the distinction between objective observation and subjective participation is not clear. "The outstanding peculiarity of this method is that the observer, in greater or less degree, is caught up in the very web of social interaction which he observes, analyzes, and reports" (Hughes, 1960, xiv). There is considerable opportunity for the participant observer to experience conflict between his or her goals as an observer and his or her goals as a participant. Review of participant observation literature indicates subjects generally respond to participant observers, in the long run, as participants (rather than observers). "Because he is a participant, even if he announces to people that he is there to study them (as I did most of the time in my fieldwork) people soon forget why he is there, and react to him as a participant" (Gans, 1968, 305). This is because the people under study view him more as a participant in their reality than a detached social scientist.

Many field researchers who have used the participant observation method report a transition and conflict between their observer and participant roles. This transition and conflict is affected, in part, by their intrapersonal perspectives on each role. The transition and conflict involves the extremes of being a stranger (observer) and being a friend (participant). Personal effects and subsequent self-concept alterations can occur within the participant observer during the involvement with the studied phenomena, even though the participant observer may be fully aware of his or her observation and participation goals. Mere exposure can manipulate, positively or negatively, the frame of reference of the participant observer. This manipulation is affected by the intrapersonal reflection that occurs.

Blanche Geer explains changes that she felt after three days of fieldwork in a college environment.

> Before entering the field, I thought of them as irresponsible children. But as I listened to their voices, learned their language, witnessed gesture and expression, and accumulated the bits of information about them which bring people alive and make their problems real, I achieved a form of empathy with them and became their advocate. (Geer, 1967, 394-395)

She reports observers who began work months later experienced the same change, but not until they entered the field. It is surprising her field notes do not indicate this change. This intrapersonal shift would be relevant to report, especially since other observers experienced it as well.

Sometimes the reports of intrapersonal perceptions are not logical, perhaps because of the complex nature of the situations being discussed. Barrie Thorne researched the draft resistance movement in Boston during the Vietnam War. Her inner conflict between her goals as a participant and as an observer are apparent within her discussion of her personal experience as a participant observer. "The conflicts I experienced between being a committed participant and an observing sociologist often took the form of great pangs of guilt, and a sense that I was betraying the movement" (Thorne, 1979, 83). It is not clear in her discussion how her observer status betrayed the movement.

Robert Bogdan reports on his field study in "Interviewing People Labeled Retarded." His study focused on mentally disabled individuals. He explains an instance where the gap between stranger (observer) and friend (participant) was bridged. "When we were told that Pattie wanted to leave the state school but had no place to go, we began looking around for a family that might be willing to provide a place for her to stay. We found a home; it was mine" (Bogdan, 1980, 240). This exemplifies a situation where the researcher has been affected intrapersonally and interpersonally.

I will now describe my research experience, regarding intrapersonal evaluations and reevaluations, using the aforementioned experiences of others as context. My first experience using the participant observation method occurred during my doctoral dissertation research. Participant observation was my primary method for data collection. The problem of the study dealt with conflict resolution communication attempts practiced by the Woodstock Food Co-op (a pseudonym). I wanted to find if the ideals of the counterculture were evidenced in the communication attempts at conflict resolution. The Co-op presented itself as being based on a countercultural philosophy and was studied as a representative organization of the counterculture. It was studied as a representative countercultural organization primarily because of the way in which it defined itself.

The data gathered during the study conveyed unexpected findings. Results indicated the Co-op only superficially practiced a countercultural philosophy. The Co-op presented itself as using a consensus process in formal situations, but analysis found it actually used a form of voting. It promoted egalitarian themes in informal situations, but analysis found it actually had a recognized hierarchy among the membership. Thus, the Co-op conveyed itself as practicing a countercultural philosophy, but analysis found it actually practiced dominant culture approaches in communication attempts at conflict resolution. Dominant culture themes were evident in other areas as well.

The hypothesis of the study was that the Co-op, as a representative organization within the counterculture, would utilize a consensus process in formal situations and practice egalitarian ideals in informal situations. The data collected during the study clearly confirmed the hypothesis was false. I was both academically and personally surprised when the data disproved my hypothesis. Nothing in my literature review or personal experience had given me indications the hypothesis might be false.

Up to the point when I realized the hypothesis was false, I had been an individual who associated himself with the counterculture and believed the counterculture offered a necessary alternative. I personally hoped there would be stronger distinctions between the counterculture and dominant culture conflict resolution communication attempts. This would have indicated a stronger distinction between the philosophies of the counterculture and dominant culture. The discovery that such strong distinctions did not exist affected my evaluation of one of my primary groups and, in turn, affected my self-concept. This fundamental shift occurred mostly through intrapersonal thought processes.

I had been involved with a variety of countercultural organizations for roughly three years before beginning the study. I associated myself with the counterculture strongly during those years, both in thought and appearance. This interest with the counterculture stemmed, in part, from my experience as a second lieutenant in the Air Force. I had been in ROTC as an undergraduate student and entered the Air Force six months after graduation. After a year in the service, I applied for (and was granted) an early release from active duty. The release was under honorable conditions and was sanctioned through an Air Force program that allowed officers to return to graduate school, but still maintain their position in reserve status. I have since reentered the active reserve and hold the rank of Lieutenant Colonel.

My initial Air Force experience was not what I anticipated. My resulting countercultural leanings were in response to the impersonal bureaucracy that I perceived during my first year in the Air Force. I did not experience disagreement with the goals of the military, rather, I experienced Roszak's explanation of the counterculture. Roszak explains counterculture as arising from a youthful revulsion at technocracy. It represents a refusal to surrender spontaneity to artificiality. The counterculture serves to reassert life and joy in the face of impersonal organization (Roszak, 1969, 2). I should note my experience as a military reservist has been very positive due to my more realistic expectations.

I concentrated on achieving as high a degree of objectivity as possible during the early months of the study. I did not want my personal countercultural leanings to influence my academic observations. I wanted the data to speak for itself and it did. My data (from observations, interviews, surveys, and review of literature written by/about the organization) indicated the countercultural base of the Co-op, and related organizations, was much more superficial than anticipated. The superficial trends existed consistently from the start of the study but were not evident to me until I evaluated the data I had collected over a period of time. This detached period of evaluation enhanced my objectivity.

My intrapersonal reflections were significantly affected by the findings derived from the data collected. The consistencies in the data encouraged me academically, but discouraged me personally. I initially questioned the sincerity of the counterculture and then began to question my future personal involvement with the counterculture. Could I better achieve my altruistic aims through a different means? I had originally identified strongly with the Co-op membership, and related organizations, but my personal orientation shifted away from this identification during the study. The shift was evidenced in my personal journal.

> My views have changed since I started the study. The distinctions between dominant culture organizations and countercultural organizations seem to be superficial. I think I can offer a more realistic contribution by working within the system than by working outside of it. Some may call it "selling out." I'll call disillusionment. The goals are still the same . . . I think I'll just try another path. (Field notes, 1982)

This personal questioning occurred, little by little, during the course of the data-gathering period, rather than through an abrupt realization.

Other researchers have reported such shifts in intrapersonal perspectives. Rosalie Wax shares a similar experience in "Final Thoughts: How Fieldwork Changed Me." "What changed me irrevocably and beyond repair were the things I learned . . . these irrevocable changes involved replacing mythical and ideological assumptions with the correct (though often painful) facts of the situation" (Wax, 1971, 363). As with Wax, what changed me irrevocably were the things I learned. These changes involved replacing personal ideological assumptions "with the correct (though often painful) facts of the situation." Again, this shift in perspective occurs primarily through the intrapersonal channel.

I have reflected on my fieldwork experience a lot since completing my participant observation study. It was academically rewarding as a Ph.D. dissertation and personally rewarding as a learning experience. My initial motivation for writing this article stemmed from an interest in learning about the personal experiences of other participant observers and to see what consistencies, if any, exist among people who have used the participant observation method. A secondary motivation has been to speculate on how researchers experience change intrapersonally and concurrently maintain necessary detachment from the environment they are studying.

Participant observation is but one of many research methods used in the social sciences. It has been used by a wide range of researchers to investigate many types of research problems. It is difficult to speculate on the psychological makeup of participant observers. A common thread that does exist within most participant observation accounts is the concern with objectivity. Not necessarily achieving total objectivity, but consistently working to maintain a high degree of it. This would require a particular ability to detach oneself periodically from one's personal frame of reference. "It is doubtful whether one can become a good social reporter unless he has been able to look, in a reporting mood, at the social world in which he was reared" (Hughes, 1960, xi) or at least be able to maintain some degree of detachment in that regard.

As a participant observer who associated himself with the counterculture, and who has done fieldwork within the counterculture, I am particularly interested in Herbert Gans discussion of fieldworkers.

> My hunch is that fieldwork attracts a person who, in Everett Hughes' words, "is alienated from his own background," who is not entirely comfortable in his new roles, or who is otherwise detached from his own society; the individual who is more comfortable as an observer than as a participant. (Gans, 1968, 317)

The alienation emphasized by Hughes parallels the alienation frequently felt within the counterculture (Roszak, 1969, 2). This alienation can obviously exist in a variety of situations and contexts outside of the counterculture.

The research process draws from a variety of methods. Each method has strengths and weaknesses. I believe concern with the personal effects of a method, in this case participant observation, is central to understanding the entire research process. "What good is a research design that does not include some reference to those who will execute it" (Hughes, 1964, 82) or who have executed it? My review of literature reveals a minimal fund of information regarding the personal effects of such research. This article is intended as encouragement for others to share the personal effects of their research experiences, how they dealt with these effects intrapersonally, and how they maintained appropriate degrees of researcher detachment throughout their research.

Notes

Bogdan, R. "Interviewing People Labeled Retarded," in W.B. Shaffir, R.A. Stebbins, and A. Turowetz, eds., *Fieldwork Experience: Qualitative Approaches to Social Research*. New York: St. Martin's Press, 1980.

Field notes. February 5, 1982. Reflections on my personal involvement as a participant observer.

Filstead, W. *Qualitative Methodology*. Chicago: Markham Publishing Co., 1970.

Gans, H.J. "The Participant Observer as a Human Being: Observations on the Personal Aspects of Fieldwork," in H.S. Becker, B. Geer, D. Riesman, and R.S. Weiss, eds., *Institutions and the Person*. Chicago: Aldine Publishing Co., 1968.

Geer, B. "First Days in the Field," in P.E. Hammond, ed. *Sociologists at Work*. Garden City, NY: Doubleday and Co., Inc., 1967.

Hughes, E.C. "French Canada: The Natural History of a Research Project," in A.J. Vidich, J. Bensman, and M.R. Stein. *Reflections on Community Studies*. New York: John Wiley and Sons, Inc., 1964.

Hughes, E.C. "Introduction," in B.H. Junker, *Fieldwork*. Chicago: The University of Chicago Press, 1960.

Jones, S.E. and A.E. Yarbrough, "A Naturalistic Study of the Meanings of Touch," *Communication Monographs*, Vol. 52, 1985, 19-56.

Owen, W.F. "Teacher Classroom Management Communication: A Qualitative Case Study," *Communication Education*, Vol. 33, 1984, 137-142.

Philipsen, G. "Speaking 'Like a Man' in Teamsterville: Culture Patterns of Role Enactment in an Urban Neighborhood," *Quarterly Journal of Speech*, Vol. 61, 1975, 21-29.

Roszak, T. *The Making of a Counterculture*. Garden City, NY: Anchor Books, 1969.

Shaffir, W.B., Stebbins R.A., and Turowetz, A. *Fieldwork Experience: Qualitative Approaches to Social Research*. New York: St. Martin's Press, 1980.

Thorne, B. "Political Activist as Participant Observer: Conflicts of Commitment in a Study of the Draft Resistance Movement of the 1960s," *Symbolic Interaction*, Vol. 2, 1979, 80-91.

Wax, R. *Doing Fieldwork: Warnings and Advice*. Chicago: University of Chicago Press, 1971.

Section Two

CASE STUDIES IN
CROSS-CULTURAL CONTEXTS

Chapter Seven

Faculty Dominance in a Group/Classroom Context: Comparing the United States and South Africa

The release of antiapartheid activist Nelson Mandela marked another step toward racial equality in South Africa. Antiapartheid reforms have been sought in practically all areas of South African life including economic, political, and educational reforms. This chapter will focus on how faculty preference for dominance in South African university classrooms hinders cross-cultural relations. Examination of South African faculty perspectives is compared and contrasted against U.S. faculty perspectives using a survey of culture bound areas. This analysis is intended to serve as an indicator of educational shortcomings, regarding cross-cultural communication in the classroom, and establish a need for modifications in this area. Before focusing on education in South Africa, a brief overview of the country will provide helpful context for the situation being reported on.

South Africa is roughly three times the size of California. Seventy-five percent of its population (of 36 million) is Black, 14 percent White, 8 percent coloureds (mixed Black/White/Asian), and 3 percent Asian and others. The chief commercial exports are gold, diamonds, uranium, platinum, chrome, and copper (Dostert, 1987, 93).

Race relations have long been controversial and, at present, much of the controversy stems from apartheid (even though it has been legally abolished). Apartheid, a Boer word meaning separate, is a policy that provides for legalized compulsory separation of the races. This policy was instituted in 1948 when the National Party came to power. During the 1960s Black rights were further reduced due to the threat posed by the African National Congress (that Nelson Mandela led). In 1973, ten Black homelands were established that allowed for internal self-government. In 1986 the United States and other countries increased sanctions against South Africa to discourage apartheid, including bans on investments, loans, South African exports into the United States, and divestment in companies that operate in South Africa (Dostert, 1987, 93-98). The sanctions were successful in helping to bring down apartheid.

I visited South Africa for two weeks during July 1989. My reason for the visit was to present a workshop on cross-cultural communication in the classroom at the annual national meeting of the South African Applied Linguistics Association. The meeting was held at the University of Natal in Durban. The University of Natal is one of five universities that has openly rejected apartheid. My visit allowed for observation of day-to-day life in South Africa. Local newspapers are full of articles and letters that give an impression of the chasm that exists between Black and White life in South Africa. In a typical letter to the editor a writer shares an opinion on segregation of public areas in Durban.

> We well remember those days when one could find a seat on a park bench where it was safe from a mugging or stabbing from layabouts; when one could stroll the Amphitheatre at night without fear of rape or worse; when libraries were quiet, pleasant places to visit without having to avoid the stretched out legs of some sleeping African; when queues in post offices were shorter; and when public toilets were fit and safe to use. (Buckman, 1989, 2)

This perspective is representative of the views expressed by many writers in South African newspapers. It is difficult to comprehend how devastating insensitivity among South Africa's racial groups must be on cross-cultural communication in the classroom. Speculation on White attitudes toward non-Whites is a primary concern in this chapter.

The Problem and Method of Investigation

Study of cross-cultural communication has increased significantly since World War II. World trade and international exchange have helped perpetuate this increase. As the classroom becomes more culturally diverse it is important that faculty consider the cultural variables that are introduced in such a situation. These variables based on the different backgrounds represented can serve as benefits to the learning process. I propose *sensitivity* with cross-cultural differences can lead to cross-cultural *awareness*, which in turn can lead to improved cross-cultural *understanding*. The order in which these elements occur may vary from individual to individual and the elements can continually reoccur in a person's development (i.e., sensitivity can lead to awareness that can lead to understanding that can lead to greater sensitivity, etc.).

Culture is the backdrop within which teaching and learning takes place. The function of culture in the communication process is developed later in this section. We all use our cultural background to "filter" what we are perceiving in the classroom. Thus, the faculty member can actually experience "culture shock" in his or her own classroom without leaving the country. Culture shock occurs when we experience confusion, anger, or despair as a result of unsuccessful attempts to make sense of cultural practices which are foreign to us. This usually occurs when we are outside of our own culture (in another country), but it can happen when dealing with culturally different individuals in our own culture. One does not need to be interested in diversity to experience culture shock. Any interaction with culturally different individuals can perpetuate culture shock (if the confusion exists).

A survey entitled "Cultural Bound Areas for Personal Reflection" is included at the end of this paper as Attachments #1, #2, and #3. These cultural bound areas are areas that can be interpreted and emphasized in significantly different ways depending upon an individual's cultural background. Thus, they can be obstacles to the learning process. The survey is based on an outline of culture bound areas that was created by the National Association of Developmental Education. I constructed the survey for the purpose of collecting data. It is in the early stages of development and does not have a rigorous foundation within the context of social science research.

This is a self-reporting instrument. Faculty indicate their responses to each statement in each area: strongly agree, agree, neutral, disagree, and strongly disagree. Again, these are areas that are frequently interpreted and emphasized differently depending on the individual's cultural background. This instrument focuses on teacher expectations, standards, personal perspectives, approaches in common situations, and how these areas can benefit or detract from the classroom environment. Some of the areas deal strongly with faculty dominance and other areas are far less related to faculty dominance. The quote by Franklin D. Roosevelt at the bottom of the survey is recognized as a possible source of bias to be felt by respondents. The quote was included because it fit the theme of the workshops where the survey was used.

Awareness of these areas is also beneficial when working with the variety of subcultures that comprise individual cultures. Misunderstandings can occur as a result of differing frames of reference. Differing frames of reference do not necessarily indicate opposite interpretations of the culture bound areas, rather they imply various interpretations on the same continuum (but differing in varying degrees depending on the cultural backgrounds compared).

Classroom cross-cultural understanding (in the United States, South Africa, or anywhere) can be enhanced through an awareness of cross-cultural communication dynamics. Cross-cultural communication "occurs when two or more individuals with different cultural backgrounds interact together. . . . In most situations intercultural interactants do not share the same language. But languages can be learned and larger communication problems occur in the nonverbal realm" (Andersen, 1986). "Since we are not usually aware of our own nonverbal behavior it becomes extremely difficult to identify and master the nonverbal behavior of another culture. At times we feel uncomfortable in other cultures because we intuitively know something isn't right" (Andersen, 1987, 2-3). "Because nonverbal behaviors are rarely conscious phenomena, it may be difficult for us to know exactly why we are feeling uncomfortable" (Gudykunst and Kim, 1984, 149).

The effect of the cultural backgrounds of interactants on human interaction is a crucial consideration. "Culture is the enduring influence of the social environment on our behavior including our interpersonal communication behaviors" (Andersen, 1987, 6). The culture of an individual dictates interpersonal behavior through "control mechanisms—plans, recipes, rules, instructions (what computer engineers call 'programs')—for the governing of behavior" (Geertz, 1973, 44). Thus, the processes for presentation of ideas (speaking) and the reception of ideas (listening) will understandably vary from culture to culture.

Different perceptions of the culture bound areas in the survey are not always a matter of differing values. Values can be similar but the expression of these values, based on cultural communicative norms, can vary significantly. Cross-cultural understanding can become especially difficult because different perceptions of culture bound areas can be a matter of differing values and differing communication processes. How faculty teach their classes can be more important (with this issue) than what we are teaching. That is, actions speak louder than words. Thus, a multicultural classroom environment that is sensitive to various cultural and subcultural backgrounds is going to help provide considerable understanding for students of all backgrounds. Obviously the faculty member has a direct influence on this classroom environment.

I have used the aforementioned survey at faculty workshops I have led, focusing on the multicultural classroom, in the United States and South Africa. Comparison and contrast of faculty responses to these survey areas can exemplify the void between United States and South African faculty perspectives (although there are similarities evidenced). The survey was used in March 1989 with 97 English/Speech/Linguistics faculty members at the annual Conference on Student Success Courses held in Orlando, Florida. The survey was also used in July 1989 with 112 English/Speech/Linguistics faculty members at the annual meeting of the South African Applied Linguistics Association held in Durban. This is obviously a very limited sample of the academic disciplines in both countries. Neither group can offer a perfect standard to evaluate other nationalities by, but comparison and contrast does highlight differences allowing for examination of why groups vary regarding cross-cultural perspectives.

Report of Data

Responses to the survey by South African faculty members are included as Attachment #1. One hundred and twelve participants were surveyed. The numbers noted on the survey are percentage responses to each area. Review of the survey responses indicates strong consistencies and a desire for faculty dominance exemplified in most areas. For instance, 87 percent prefer formal communication rather than informal communication with students, 90 percent state they never lose control over the classroom, 72 percent prefer docile students, 89 percent feel respect for authority is important, 78 percent consider dress and cleanliness as important, and 84 percent state cheating should result in expulsion.

Responses to the survey by American faculty members are included as Attachment #2. Ninety-seven participants were surveyed. The numbers noted on the survey are percentage responses to each area. Review of these survey responses, in contrast with the South African responses, indicates considerable diversity regarding faculty perspectives on the culture bound areas and less preference for faculty dominance. American society is a diverse culture. Perhaps this cultural diversity is a base for the diverse interpretations noted in the survey. Again, it is important to remember there are not correct or incorrect responses to survey areas. The survey merely gauges respondent perspectives as they relate to cultural norms.

Attachment #3 compares and contrasts responses by U.S. and South African respondents. As noted at the top of the survey, American majority responses are indicated with an **x** and South African majority responses are indicated with an **o**. Review of these responses indicates similarities and differences between the two groups. Most notable are four areas that show radically different perspectives. These are I.A. (teacher-student communication should be formal), I.F. (cheating should result in expulsion), III.A. (importance of treating students the same), and III.C. (preference for docile students). It is interesting to acknowledge that both groups agree respect for authority is important (I.E.). These are the significant findings drawn from the survey data.

I am cautious not to overanalyze the data collected for fear of drawing conclusions that are not accurate. The purpose of using this survey is to learn about general perspectives that exist in both populations studied. It is not intended to be a comprehensive database. I am in search of general agreement or disagreement readings regarding the survey statements.

In each of the areas where responses differed, the South African group differed in favor of faculty dominance in the classroom. This general finding can be realized without statistical correlation by merely reviewing survey response percentages. South African faculty indicated teacher-student communication should be formal, student cheating should result in expulsion, it is not necessary to treat students the same, and a preference for docile students.

In contrast, the American group indicated teacher-student communication should be informal, student cheating should not result in expulsion, it is necessary to treat students the same, and a preference for aggressive students. Even in areas where both groups agreed, the South African group indicated stronger faculty dominance. In area I.E., 70 percent of the American respondents felt respect for authority was important compared to 89 percent of the South African respondents who felt respect for authority was important.

The sample populations used in this study are not large enough or representative enough to be statistically analyzed for tendencies and correlations. The comparison of cross-cultural preferences that exist in two distinctly different cultural settings is the first step toward the larger task of quantification and measurement of effects of these preferences.

Discussion

Using faculty members as an indicator, and based on the information gathered with this survey, South African faculty members prefer more dominance in the classroom (when compared with the U.S. academic community). Faculty members who teach English, Speech, and Linguistics in both cultures have been used as representative samples to generalize faculty perceptions regarding survey areas. I contend the South African emphasis on faculty dominance can negatively affect cross-cultural relations in the classroom (although this cannot be accurately assumed in all situations). A faculty member who exercises dominance in the classroom will be stressing control using his or her cultural perspective as a frame of reference (regardless of other cultural frames of reference of students).

I am asserting, in the context of this chapter, that a preference for control in the classroom is correlated with a preference for dominance and a permissive teaching style is correlated with a sensitivity for diversity. This is not to say a professor with a dominant teaching style cannot allow diversity. The aforementioned assertion rests on the belief that the promotion of sensitivity with diversity generally begins with an individual who maintains a permissive perspective toward new and different ideas (that could inhibit his or her control of the classroom).

In *Racial and Ethnic Groups*, Schaefer (1990) describes the consequences of minority status as a result of majority control. These consequences are: 1) extermination, 2) expulsion, 3) secession, 4) segregation, 5) fusion, 6) assimilation, and 7) pluralism (36-39). These consequences build from extreme intolerance to tolerance. Similarly, these consequences build from extreme dominance by the controlling dominant group to higher degrees of permissiveness by the controlling dominant group.

Fourteen percent of the South African population is White, yet 98.2 percent of the faculty surveyed in this study are White. Therefore, the White South African cultural perspective will be the dominant cultural perspective in 98.2 percent of the university classrooms, assuming this sample is representative, while only 14 percent of the population shares this cultural perspective. Therefore, many university students are judged by faculty members who use a cultural perspective (in a dominant manner) different than their own.

The United States and South Africa have cultural diversity but the main difference is that South Africa has far less interaction among their culturally different populations. Segregation in public accommodations, education, housing, etc., is legislated against in the United States while segregation (apartheid) is legislated in South Africa. I believe *separation* among racial groups leads to *ignorance* about other racial groups, which leads to *fear* of other racial groups. A symptom of this problem in South Africa is the institution of apartheid.

Alex Boraine, executive director of the Institute for a Democratic Alternative for South Africa, summarized a similar view in the South African press. "Many White South Africans have genuine deep-rooted fears . . . the causes of such fears were largely attributable to widespread ignorance of black people. . . . Whites and Blacks for the most part live in different worlds, and isolation breeds ignorance, which brings with it fear" (Boraine, 1989, 3).

Conclusions

The United States has progressed significantly towards improvement of cross-cultural relations in and out of the classroom. I contend we are ahead of South Africa in this area because there is less separation of culturally different people in the United States. Thus, it will benefit the United States to continue to promote interaction among culturally different people. "Projections indicate that ethnic and racial minorities will compose one-third of the U.S. population by the year 2000 and 45 percent by 2050" (Friedrich, 1989, 3). The United States will do well to emphasize interaction-knowledge-understanding (rather than separation-ignorance-fear).

Emphasis on sensitivity among cultures can be found in classroom considerations for the future. J. Jeffery Auer, a well-recognized leader in the speech communication field, states "Displaying tolerance requires only patience while the other cultural minority does or says its thing. But accepting cultural pluralism requires a real effort to understand other cultural entities, to listen to what they say, and appreciate the context from which they speak" (Auer, 1989). Regarding curriculum development, "specific cultures of minority students should be considered when planning curricula, teaching speech classes, and conducting teaching training programs" (Atwater, 1989).

In conclusion, South African survey responses indicate a general preference for faculty dominance (compared to U.S. diversity and permissiveness). A reason for these differences could be that enhanced cross-cultural interaction in the United States gives us constant reminders there are different cultural perspectives than those held by our own cultural group. South Africa does not have this reminder because they have less interaction among culturally different people.

As long as this condition exists in South Africa the communicative climate in the classroom will surely suffer as a result of negative cross-cultural relations. Awareness can be the first step toward social change. I contend South African faculty can promote positive social change through emphasis on cross-cultural sensitivity in their classrooms.

Notes

Andersen, P.A. "Consciousness, Cognition, and Communication," *Western Journal of Speech Communication*, 50 (1986), 87-101.

Andersen, P.A. "Explaining Intercultural Differences in Nonverbal Communication." Paper presented at the annual meeting of the Speech Communication Association, Boston, MA , November 1987.

Atwater, D.F. "Issues Facing Minorities in Speech Communication Education: Moving from the Melting Pot to a Tossed Salad." A presentation at the Eastern Communication Association Convention, Ocean City, MD, May 5, 1989.

Auer, J.J. "Pride in Our Past, Faith in Our Future." Conference address at the Central States Communication Association Convention, Kansas City, KS, April 14, 1989.

Boraine, A. "Whites Fears of the Future Cannot be Ignored," *Natal Mercury* (July 7, 1989), 3.

Buckman, F.H. "Those Old Days Remembered," *Natal Mercury* (July 8, 1989), 2.

Dostert, E. *The World Today Series: Africa 1987*. Washington, D.C.: Stryker-Post Publications, 1987.

Friedrich, G.W. "Make Mine a Tossed Salad," *SPECTRA* (December 1989), 3.

Geertz, C. *The Interpretation of Cultures*. New York: Basic Books, 1973.

Gudykunst, W.B. and Kim, Y.Y. *Communicating with Strangers: An Approach to Intercultural Communication*. New York: Random House, 1984.

Schaefer, R.T. *Racial and Ethnic Groups*. Glenview, IL: Scott Foresman Co., 1990.

Attachment #1

112 SOUTH AFRICAN FACULTY (stated in %)

SA—strongly agree   A—agree   N—neutral
D—disagree   SD—strongly disagree

CULTURAL BOUND AREAS FOR PERSONAL REFLECTION:

I. EXPECTATIONS AND STANDARDS	SA	A	N	D	SD
A. Teacher-student communication should be based on formal (rather than informal) interaction.	5 16	4 71	3 4	2 5	1 4
B. Dress and cleanliness is important.	5 23	4 55	3 7	2 10	1 5
C. If a student is academically unprepared, it is primarily his or her own fault.	5 33	4 56	3 1	2 7	1 3
D. Students should have a lot of free time.	5 2	4 5	3 18	2 58	1 17
E. Respect for authority is important.	5 37	4 52	3 8	2 3	1
F. If a student is caught in an academically dishonest action, he or she should be expelled from school.	5 26	4 58	3 2	2 12	1 2

II. APPROACHES	SA	A	N	D	SD
A. I handle emotionally charged issues and conflict by never losing control of myself or my control over the classroom.	5 14	4 76	3 6	2 4	1
B. Humor is essential in the classroom.	5 5	4 50	3 3	2 33	1 9
C. I enjoy some students less than others.	5 20	4 44	3 13	2 17	1 6

III. PREFERENCES

	SA	A	N	D	SD
A. It is important for me to treat students the same. They should never know if I really like them individually or not.	5 **12**	4 **13**	3 **6**	2 **47**	1 **22**
B. I prefer group (instead of individual) learning activities.	5 **6**	4 **6**	3 **12**	2 **58**	1 **18**
C. I prefer docile (instead of aggressive) students.	5 **7**	4 **65**	3 **8**	2 **13**	1 **7**

"Today we are faced with the preeminent fact that, if civilization is to survive, we must cultivate the science of human relationships—the ability of all peoples, of all kinds, to live together and work together, in the same world, at peace."

Franklin D. Roosevelt
(April 13, 1945)

Attachment #2

97 AMERICAN FACULTY (stated in %)

SA—strongly agree   A—agree   N—neutral
D—disagree   SD—strongly disagree

CULTURAL BOUND AREAS FOR PERSONAL REFLECTION:

I. EXPECTATIONS AND STANDARDS

	SA	A	N	D	SD
A. Teacher-student communication should be based on formal (rather than informal) interaction.	5 **8**	4 **22**	3	2 **55**	1 **15**
B. Dress and cleanliness is important.	5 **6**	4 **23**	3 **45**	2 **5**	1 **11**
C. If a student is academically unprepared, it is primarily his or her own fault.	5 **5**	4 **44**	3 **20**	2 **25**	1 **6**
D. Students should have a lot of free time.	5 **11**	4 **30**	3 **14**	2 **43**	1 **2**

	SA	A	N	D	SD
E. Respect for authority is important.	5	4	3	2	1
	11	**59**	**23**	**7**	
F. If a student is caught in an academically dishonest action, he or she should be expelled from school.	5	4	3	2	1
	9	**36**	**11**	**41**	**3**

II. APPROACHES

	SA	A	N	D	SD
A. I handle emotionally charged issues and conflict by never losing control of myself or my control over the classroom.	5	4	3	2	1
	2	**81**	**4**	**13**	
B. Humor is essential in the classroom.	5	4	3	2	1
	14	**38**	**15**	**31**	**3**
C. I enjoy some students less than others.	5	4	3	2	1
	19	**65**	**2**	**14**	

III. PREFERENCES

	SA	A	N	D	SD
A. It is important for me to treat students the same. They should never know if I really like them individually or not.	5	4	3	2	1
	32	**36**		**29**	**3**
B. I prefer group (instead of individual) individual) learning activities.	5	4	3	2	1
	6	**29**	**7**	**51**	**7**
C. I prefer docile (instead of aggressive) students.	5	4	3	2	1
	4	**30**	**22**	**37**	**7**

"Today we are faced with the preeminent fact that, if civilization is to survive, we must cultivate the science of human relationships—the ability of all peoples, of all kinds, to live together and work together, in the same world, at peace."

Franklin D. Roosevelt
(April 13, 1945)

Attachment #3

AMERICAN FACULTY(x)
SOUTH AFRICAN FACULTY(o)

SA—strongly agree   A—agree   N—neutral
D—disagree   SD—strongly disagree

CULTURAL BOUND AREAS FOR PERSONAL REFLECTION:

I. EXPECTATIONS AND STANDARDS	SA	A	N	D	SD
A. Teacher-student communication should be based on formal (rather than informal) interaction.	5	4 o	3	2 x	1
B. Dress and cleanliness is important.	5	4 o	3 x	2	1
C. If a student is academically unprepared, it is primarily his or her own fault.	5	4 xo	3	2	1
D. Students should have a lot of free time.	5	4	3	2 xo	1
E. Respect for authority is important.	5	4 xo	3	2	1
F. If a student is caught in an academically dishonest action, he or she should be expelled from school.	5	4 o	3	2 x	1

II. APPROACHES	SA	A	N	D	SD
A. I handle emotionally charged issues and conflict by never losing control of myself or my control over the classroom.	5	4 xo	3	2	1
B. Humor is essential in the classroom.	5	4 xo	3	2	1
C. I enjoy some students less than others.	5	4 xo	3	2	1

III. PREFERENCES

	SA	A	N	D	SD

A. It is important for me to treat students the
same. They should never know if I really
like them individually or not.

	5	4	3	2	1
		x		o	

B. I prefer group (instead of individual) learning
activities.

	5	4	3	2	1
		xo			

C. I prefer docile (instead of aggressive) students.

	5	4	3	2	1
		o		x	

"Today we are faced with the preeminent fact that, if civilization is to survive, we must cultivate the science of human relationships—the ability of all peoples, of all kinds, to live together and work together, in the same world, at peace."

Franklin D. Roosevelt
(April 13, 1945)

Chapter Eight

Seeking Human Communication Perspectives, Espoused by a Marginalized Group, to Perpetuate a More Inclusive Curriculum

The education curriculum is never finished. It is dynamic and continually in a state of change. This chapter focuses on the use of research findings by African American scholars to expand the communication arts curriculum as a means of reshaping the curriculum so it is more representative of the various cultures that compose U.S. society. This move towards a more multicultural curriculum should focus on all U.S. cultural backgrounds. This chapter addresses contributions by African American scholars but is intended to provide a framework for inclusion of other underrepresented cultures in the United States (i.e., Asian American, Latino American, etc.).

Roughly 33 percent of school-age children in the United States are of non-European origin (*Learn about Diversity*, 1993, 4). Thus, we have a unique opportunity and obligation to ensure our academic curriculums are representative of these non-European perspectives. Thorough modifications will be a lengthy process. Calls for a more inclusive curriculum representative of the multicultural composition of American society have come from a variety of sources (Williams, 1990; Viadero, 1992; Gordon and Bhattacharyya, 1992). One frequently hears that we need emphasis on education as a means to help American society get along with itself (in the area of interracial/ethnic relations). Common sense supports an inclusive curriculum representative of the many cultural groups that comprise the United States that will appeal to the diverse audience educated in the United States.

This chapter focuses on the use of research findings by African American scholars to expand the communication studies curriculum. The aforementioned inclusive curriculum can obviously only be attained when scholarship representative of all American cultures is included in curriculum expansion efforts. Emphasis on African American scholars within this chapter is intended as one of many steps towards an inclusive curriculum. And, obviously, communication studies is but one of many disciplines to be expanded.

A review of literature on the subject of curriculum development and multicultural inclusiveness reveals little that deals with models for curricular development specifically in communication studies. However, much has been written on curriculum development and multicultural inclusiveness that can be applied in communication studies and other disciplines within the social sciences. Helle Bering-Jensen (1990) recommends inclusion of minority contributions in classroom content as a means of supplementing Eurocentric perspectives. Beverly Tatum (1992) offers strategies for overcoming student resistance to race-related content. Emphasis on inclusion of culturally diverse works of literature is described in Pfordresher (1992) and Post (1992). Michael Harris (1992) suggests one means of addressing racial problems is to promote inclusion of African and African American content in U.S. public schools. Kerry Feldman (1992) emphasizes how anthropology departments can be helpful in choosing multicultural education components. Jerry Gaff (1992) claims that multiculturalism has won the war against Eurocentrism and that we should move to the next step of creating inclusive programs that are educationally valuable.

These views point to the need for expansion of the curriculum. Again, the focus of this article is on the inclusion of African American scholarship as an initial objective, with the inclusion of scholarship representative of all American cultures being the primary long-term objective.

During the past quarter century many colleges and universities have tried to include minorities in their curriculums through the creation of African American studies departments that stress Black contributions. It is a central premise of the Lilly Foundation grant proposal that funded the research undertaken by me at this time that "If majority students are to gain the benefits of the minority perspectives, we believe that the contributions of minorities should claim their proper place throughout the curriculum and not be relegated to a 'separate but distinct' area" (Ohio Dominican University, 1991, 13).

I have approached my research of African American scholarship as an opportunity to substantively augment my academic orientation. One could merely use a recipe approach of "just add African American readings and stir," but this would only allow for cosmetic changes. Rather, I have approached this as I did when learning new material in graduate school. Knowledge learned is intended to become part of my theoretical fabric. Such an approach takes time and thorough analysis. My graduate training was a long, in-depth period of study. Any serious modifications of that foundation will come through a similar path.

The communication studies discipline covers a wide range of subject areas including public speaking, interpersonal communication, organizational communication, mass media, rhetoric, journalism, public relations, broadcasting, theater, and cross-cultural studies. I have focused on five courses I teach: Rhetorical Communication Theory, Mass Media in America, Persuasion, Communication in the Organization, and a Unity in Diversity course. A majority of the works are most appropriate in the Unity in Diversity course. Examples of course modifications will be described to exemplify how curricular change in communication studies can be perpetuated.

Before addressing specific course modifications, it will be helpful to describe the process through which I gathered contributions of African American scholars. Essential in this process were my visits to the Moorland-Spingarn Research Center at Howard University. It is the "largest and the most valuable research library in America for the study of Negro life and history" and "the most comprehensive and interesting group of books by Negroes ever collected in the world" (*The Arthur B. Spingarn Collection of Negro Authors*, 1947, 1 and 7). Such a comprehensive collection of African American scholarship offers a unique opportunity to study African American contributions in a variety of areas.

I used a variety of key words to search for information relevant to communication studies. The seven most useful key words were rhetoric, communication, narration, persuasion, political oratory, nonverbal communication, and interpersonal relations. The following lists in parentheses the number of relevant titles found under each key word heading: rhetoric (36), communication (75), narration (71), persuasion (6), political oratory (7), nonverbal communication (17), and interpersonal relations (35).

Rhetorical Communication Theory is an upper-level course at Ohio Dominican University. The course traces the development of rhetoric from the classical period to the British period to the contemporary period. Two primary assignments in the course are a research paper on a significant rhetorician and an oral presentation in class about the rhetorician researched. The suggested list of rhetoricians includes individuals representing a variety of perspectives. No African Americans are included in the list. As a result, the following African American names have been added to the list as possible rhetoricians to be studied: W.E.B. DuBois, Sterling Brown, Ralph Ellison, and Toni Morrison. Thus, the list is more inclusive of afrocentric perspectives.

Students choosing to study the African American rhetoricians might use as a foundation for their research works such as *The Anatomy of Black Rhetoric* (Payne, 1982), *A Comparative Study of Two Approaches for Analyzing Black Discourse* (Phillips, 1983), *Rhetoric of Racial Hope* (Hill, 1976), *The Relationship Between Errors in Standard Usage in Written Compositions of College Students and the Students' Cognitive Styles* (Cooper, 1979), *From Behind the Veil: A Study of African-American Narrative* (Stepto, 1979), and *Black Communication* (Mullen, 1982). These works authored by African American writers focus on African American rhetoric.

The Mass Media in America course uses a textbook entitled *Introduction to Mass Media* (Black and Bryant, 1992). It can be supplemented with *Split Image* (Dates and Barlow, 1990) and *Mass Media in America* (Pember, 1992). These works better highlight the role of African Americans in mass media. Other sources regarding the role of African Americans are found in an extensive bibliography entitled *"Blacks in the Media: Communications Research Since 1978"* (Williams, 1990), published by the Howard University Center for Communications Research.

The Persuasion course describes persuasion theory and contemporary applications of persuasion theory. One of these applications involves persuasion in public speaking. Contemporary public speakers can be used for case study analysis in the course. This is an excellent opportunity to promote inclusion of African Americans (i.e., the Jesse Jackson address at the 1988 Democratic National Convention).

The Communication in the Organization course emphasizes communication in interpersonal, group, and organizational settings. One simple guideline for text selection in such a course is to review possible textbooks regarding favorable inclusion of various American subcultures in case studies, examples, photographs, and overall content. This guideline, while not a primary guideline because it does not address theoretical content, would obviously be beneficial when considering textbooks for other courses in the communication studies curriculum as well.

The Unity in Diversity course was developed under the auspices of the aforementioned Lilly grant. This course is team taught by Imali Abala (a Black female) and Jim Schnell (a White male). The course developed by Abala and Schnell is an introductory course that explores the implications of belonging to a culturally pluralistic society with all of its richness, complexities, challenges, and responsibilities. The course seeks to enhance the ability of students to interact with culturally different individuals who comprise American society. There is no textbook for the course. Instead, a readings booklet (comprised of many types of articles) has been compiled.

There are a variety of sources by Black authors relevant for study in the Unity in Diversity course. Such references include *Handbook of Intercultural Communication* (Asante, Newmark, and Blake, 1979) and *African American Communications* (Ward, 1991). These works offer perspectives on the complexities of communication among American cultures and can be helpful in enhancing student understanding of relevant considerations. Unity in Diversity is an experimental course at the time of this writing. It has the potential for being added to the core requirement courses required for all students.

A common objective in all of these courses regarding inclusion of African American perspectives is to empower students to discover African American contributions and share their discoveries in class. This allows for the individual student to learn, his or her fellow classmates to learn, and the professor to learn. This empowerment is preferable to an approach that is driven soley by the faculty member. To empower the student to learn the process for discovering African American contribution allows for more self-initiated learning by the student.

Regarding my own learning in this matter, I have begun my next step with research on an article to be titled "In Search of Afrocentric Perspectives on Human Communication." This study is intended to go further in seeking human communication theories developed by African American scholars that provide a unique African American perspective. Thus far I have found scholarship produced by African Americans but little that is particularly African American in its orientation. It is my intent in this new search to find such contributions.

Future curricular development will benefit from increased inclusion of other cultural perspectives. These perspectives obviously exist in the communication studies curriculum but, perhaps, not to the degree that they should. The modification process described in this article is offered as a model for future development regarding a more multicultural curriculum.

Notes

Asante, Molefi Kete, Newmark, Eileen, and Blake, Cecil. *Handbook of Intercultural Communication*. Beverly Hills, CA: Sage Publishers, 1979.

Bering-Jensen, Helle. "Teaching All Things to All People," *Insight*, Vol. 6, Issue 14 (April 2, 1990), 49-51.

Black, Jay and Bryant, Jennings. *Introduction to Mass Communication*. Dubuque, IA: Wm. C. Brown, 1992.

Cooper, Grace C. *The Relationship Between Errors in Standard Usage in Written Compositions of College Students and the Students' Cognitive Styles*. Dissertation, Howard University, 1979.

Dates, Jannette and Barlow, William. *Split Image: African-Americans in the Mass Media*. Washington, D.C.: Howard University Press, 1990.

Feldman, Kerry D. "Multicultural Education and Anthropology: 'The Rise of Civilization' as a Foundation Course," *Human Organization*, Vol. 51, Issue 2 (Summer, 1992), 185-186.

Gaff, Jerry G. "Beyond Politics," *Change*, Vol. 24, Issue 1 (January 1992), 30-35.

Gordon, Edmund W. and Bhattacharyya, Maitrayee. "Human Diversity, Cultural Hegemony, and the Integrity of the Academic Canon," *Journal of Negro Education*, Vol. 61, Issue 3 (Summer, 1992), 405-418.

Harris, Michael D. "Afrocentrism and Curriculum: Concepts, Issues, and Prospects," *Journal of Negro Education*, Vol. 61, Issue 3, (Summer, 1992), 301-316.

Hill, Roy L. *Rhetoric of Racial Hope*. Brockport, NY: McDaniel Press, 1976.

Learn about Diversity. South Deerfield, MA: Channing L. Bete Co., 1993.

Mullen, Robert. *Black Communication*. Lanham, MD: University Press of America, 1982.

Ohio Dominican University. "Improving Multicultural Climate at a Four-Year College," (1991). A grant proposal funded by the Lilly Foundation.

Payne, James C. *The Anatomy of Black Rhetoric*. Tallahassee, FL: Graphic Communications Associates, 1982.

Pember, Donald. *Mass Media in America*. New York: MacMillan Publishing Co., 1992.

Pfordresher, John. "Better and Different Literature in Our Time," *Design for Arts in Education*, Vol. 93, Issue 4 (March 1992), 2-10.

Phillips, Leon C. *A Comparative Study of Two Approaches for Analyzing Black Discourse*. Dissertation, Howard University, 1983.

Post, David. "Through Joshua Gap: Curricular Control and the Constructed Community," *Teachers College Record*, Vol. 93, Issue 4 (Summer, 1992), 673-696.

Stepto, Robert B. *From Behind the Veil: A Study of African-American Narrative*. Chicago: University of Illinois Press, 1979.

Tatum, Beverly Daniel. "Talking About Race, Learning About Racism: The Application of Racial Identity Development Theory in the Classroom," *Harvard Educational Review*, Vol. 62, Issue 1 (February 1992), 1-24.

The Arthur B. Spingarn Collection of Negro Authors. Washington, D.C.: Moorland Foundation, Howard University Library, n.d. (ca. 1947).

Viadero, Debra. "Issue of Multiculturalism Dominates Standards Debate," *Education Week*, Vol. 11, Issue 31 (April 22, 1992), 18.

Ward, James. *African-American Communications: An Anthology in Traditional and Contemporary Studies*. Dubuque, IA: Kendall/Hunt Publishing, 1991.

Williams, Michael A. *Blacks and the Media: Communication Research Since 1978*. Washington, D.C.: Howard University, 1990.

Chapter Nine

Gauging Your Cross-Cultural Sensitivity in Group/Classroom Contexts

"Today we are faced with the preeminent fact that, if civilization is to survive, we must cultivate the science of human relationships—the ability of all peoples, of all kinds, to live together and work together, in the same world, at peace."
Franklin D. Roosevelt
April 13, 1945

The typical American classroom in higher education has changed significantly over the past thirty years. Increased world trade has brought an influx of international students to study at American colleges and universities. The civil rights movement and educational reform in the United States have drastically increased the number of American minority students who have gone on to college. Both situations have caused a need for greater sensitivity of cross-cultural concerns in the multicultural classroom. The former situation emphasizing cultural differences and the latter situation emphasizing subcultural differences.

The primary objective of this chapter is to help faculty evaluate cross-cultural awareness in the classroom and to provide a starting point for improvement in this area (but not necessarily indicate "right/wrong" approaches). This end is stressed through the use of a self-reporting instrument that faculty can use to gauge their awareness of primary areas of cross-cultural difference in the classroom.

The survey that follows is entitled "Cultural Bound Areas for Personal Reflection." These culture bound areas are areas that can be interpreted and emphasized in significantly different ways depending upon an individual's cultural background. The survey is based on an outline of culture bound areas that was created by the National Association for Developmental Education.

SA—strongly agree
A—agree
N—neutral
D—disagree
SD—strongly disagree

CULTURAL BOUND AREAS FOR PERSONAL REFLECTION:

I. EXPECTATIONS AND STANDARDS	**SA**	**A**	**N**	**D**	**SD**
A. Teacher-student communication should be based on formal (rather than informal) interaction.	5	4	3	2	1
B. Dress and cleanliness is important.	5	4	3	2	1
C. If a student is academically unprepared, it is primarily his or her own fault.	5	4	3	2	1
D. Students should have a lot of free time.	5	4	3	2	1
E. Respect for authority is important.	5	4	3	2	1
F. If a student is caught in an academically dishonest action, he or she should be expelled from school.	5	4	3	2	1

II. APPROACHES	**SA**	**A**	**N**	**D**	**SD**
A. I handle emotionally charged issues and conflict by never losing control of myself or my control over the classroom.	5	4	3	2	1
B. Humor is essential in the classroom.	5	4	3	2	1
C. I enjoy some students less than others.	5	4	3	2	1

III. PREFERENCES	**SA**	**A**	**N**	**D**	**SD**
A. It is important for me to treat students the same. They should never know if I really like them individually or not.	5	4	3	2	1
B. I prefer group (instead of individual) learning activities.	5	4	3	2	1
C. I prefer docile (instead of aggressive) students.	5	4	3	2	1

This questionnaire is intended for use by the individual. The respondent indicates his or her response in each of the areas: strongly agree, agree, neutral, disagree, and strongly disagree. These are areas where the cultural background of each individual will impact his or her perception regarding the perspective to be maintained.

When used in a workshop setting, this survey can help participants gauge their cross-cultural sensitivity by comparing/contrasting their perceptions with others. This instrument focuses on teacher expectations, standards, personal perspectives, approaches in common situations, and how these areas can benefit or detract from the classroom environment. Use of the instrument can be prefaced with a description of theoretical concerns that underscore the relevance of areas to be reviewed. Primary benefits from this experience can be realized through discussion of how participants can use the self-assessment results to improve their teaching approaches based on increased awareness of varying cross-cultural perspectives that frequently exist in the multicultural classroom.

These are areas that are commonly misunderstood among faculty members and international students. Thus the survey can benefit users via enhanced awareness of these potential areas of misunderstanding. For instance, I.F. states "If a student is caught in an academically dishonest action, he or she should be expelled from school." This can be problematic because what is "academically dishonest in one culture may not be perceived the same way in another culture.

For instance, plagiarism in the American culture is a serious offense that can result in expulsion from school. Plagiarism in China, in general terms, is more commonly practiced since "no one owns an idea as their very own." Thus, books are more frequently copied from since "ideas belong to the masses." At first glance this would seem unethical but a closer look reveals it is not the case. The Chinese author is not necessarily claiming ideas that are not footnoted as his or her own. Nor would he or she be too concerned if his or her ideas were conveyed without footnote. Ideas are phenomena that more freely belong to all in China. In the United States we tend to see ideas more as something to be owned.

Sensitivity with these areas is helpful when interacting with the many subcultures that exist in the United States. The misunderstandings that occur among international cultures parallel the misunderstandings that exist among American subcultures. The differing frames of reference are a key variable in such interactions. These varied frames of reference reveal varied interpretations on a single continuum rather than opposite perceptions of the culture bound areas. The key here is that the degrees of difference depend on the cultural backgrounds that are compared.

There has been a marked increase of racism on college campuses across the United States. These situations have generally involved blatant actions exhibiting little, if any, understanding of cultural backgrounds other than dominant culture White America. Although this is a serious problem, and one that could become worse before it improves, we obviously cannot focus total attention on it in our classrooms. But, how we teach our classes can be more important (with this issue) than what we are teaching. That is, actions speak louder than words. Thus, a multicultural classroom environment that is sensitive to various cultural and subcultural backgrounds is going to help provide considerable understanding for students of all backgrounds. Obviously the faculty member has a direct influence on this classroom environment.

Culture is the backdrop within which teaching and learning takes place. We all use our cultural background to "filter" what we are perceiving in the classroom. Thus, the American faculty member can actually experience "culture shock" in his or her own classroom without leaving the country.

Culture shock occurs when we experience confusion, anger, or despair as a result of unsuccessful attempts to make sense of cultural practices which are foreign to us. This usually occurs when we are outside of our own culture (in another country) but it can happen when dealing with culturally different individuals in our own culture. Culture shock usually involves four stages: the honeymoon, crisis, recovery, and adjustment stages.

The honeymoon stage occurs during our initial interactions with a new culture when we are intrigued with new places and new ways of living. The crisis stage occurs when we encounter a situation that we do not know how to resolve and we become frustrated. The recovery stage occurs when we learn how to resolve the situation. The adjustment stage occurs after we have resolved the conflict and begin to enjoy the culture again.

The aforementioned situation involving differing views on academic dishonesty (between the United States and China) exemplifies a culture shock situation I experienced while teaching in China. First, I enjoyed learning new things about the Chinese culture (honeymoon). Second, I observed students plagiarizing from outside sources when writing their papers (crisis). Third, I found plagiarism is a more common practice in Chinese universities (recovery). Fourth, I told my students this was against the way I had been trained in the United States but that I would adopt the Chinese approach on the issue since I was in China (adjustment).

I have experienced paralleled situations in the United States when working with culturally different students. The following four steps describe such a case. First, I had two Vietnamese students who were new to the United States. I was interested in getting to know them as I am interested in Vietnamese history and they were "boat people" who had escaped from Vietnam (honeymoon). Second, their understanding of American culture was minimal and they had great difficulty understanding various assignments in the classroom (crisis). Third, I modified their assignments, basing them on universal understandings, so the Vietnamese students could complete the course objectives (recovery). Fourth, the students and I achieved an academic basis for common understanding (adjustment).

There are many rules of interpersonal interaction to acknowledge when considering cross-cultural communication. One such model involves high-context communication processes and low-context communication processes. In high-context cultures speakers present messages indirectly and let meanings evolve. Much is communicated through paralanguage cues and gesturing. High-context cultures are located mainly in the Orient.

Speakers in low-context cultures are more direct when presenting messages. Low-context cultures are found mainly in the United States and European countries. Awareness of these perspectives is based heavily on both verbal and nonverbal behaviors. Obviously there is much room for confusion and incorrect interpretation of intentions.

Different perceptions of the culture bound areas are not always a matter of differing values. Values can be similar but the *expression* of these values based on cultural communicative norms can vary significantly. Cross-cultural understanding can become especially difficult because different perceptions of culture bound areas can be a matter of differing values and differing communication processes. Thus, a high degree of tolerance is beneficial.

It is a myth to believe it is enough to treat culturally (or subculturally) different students like they are from your own culture (or subculture). Such a view is too ethnocentric. A basic goal can be to create a classroom environment that meets culturally different students "halfway." Intentions to establish a clear understanding can serve as a base for clear understanding. The following recommendations, general and specific, can help enhance such intentions.

Generally speaking, awareness of the affective, cognitive, and interpersonal domains of cross-cultural interaction can provide a general basis for improved relations. The affective domain involves acceptance and respect of other cultural backgrounds. The cognitive domain emphasizes knowledge and understanding of other cultural backgrounds. The interpersonal domain stresses the development of communication skills for interacting with various cultural backgrounds.

A specific approach starts with faculty members tape recording their lectures for personal review. Particular areas for evaluation include the use of sarcasm, language norms, vocal animation, supporting statements through repetition and substantiation, level of vocabulary, pronunciation and articulation, and rate of speech. All of these areas can be variables in cross-cultural interaction.

Specific analysis of the following survey areas can also be beneficial:

I.   A. Teacher-student communication should be based on formal (rather than informal) interaction.
II.   A. I handle emotionally charged issues and conflict by never losing control of myself or my control over the classroom.
II.   B. Humor is essential in the classroom.
III.   A. It is important for me to treat students the same. They should never know if I really like them individually or not.

These areas can be evaluated using taped lectures. Again, it is important to realize these areas can vary from culture to culture. In doing this type of evaluation one should consider how his or her approach fits within his or her own culture/subculture and how his or her approach could possibly conflict with other cultural/subcultural approaches.

The need for cross-cultural sensitivity in the multicultural classroom is a need that will doubtfully ever be met. But evaluation of faculty awareness in this area is the first step towards gauging our weaknesses (and strengths) regarding how we can promote a better understanding of not just what we teach but how we teach it.

Chapter Ten

Enhancing the Group Learning Experience by Weaving Multicultural Themes into the Curriculum

The multicultural framework of the United States offers unique challenges, benefits, and responsibilities. We are a nation of people whose roots represent cultures from around the world. We are challenged with the necessity to get along, benefited by the richness of our blending (but still unique) cultural backgrounds, and responsible for working together to ensure the challenge of getting along does not override the benefit of appreciating those who are culturally different from ourselves. It is in the spirit of working together that this activity is presented.

This chapter emphasizes working together to arrive at a more inclusive communication studies curriculum but it should be remembered paralleled approaches can be used in other disciplines. The issues being addressed exist across the curriculum. This is a framework of collaboration that also implies ramifications for areas beyond the classroom.

Review of relevant literature reveals the need for a more inclusive curriculum that reflects the composition of American society (Taylor 1991; Viadero, 1992; Dates, 1991; Gordon and Bhattacharyya, 1992). This need rests on the realization that roughly 33 percent of school-age children in the United States are from culturally and linguistically diverse populations that traditionally have been underrepresented or underrepresented in media industries and in media studies in higher education. There are periodic calls for education to help American society get along better with itself (regarding interracial/ethnic relations). Thus an inclusive curriculum representative of the sub-cultural groups that compose the United States is going to have more appeal with the diverse U.S. audience.

The aforementioned strategy for promoting a more inclusive communication curriculum is based on collaboration between two faculty members from two institutions. Janette Dates (an African American female) is an Associate Professor of Communication and Dean of the School of Communication at Howard University. Jim Schnell (a European American male) is a Full Professor of Communication at Ohio Dominican University. They were brought together through a grant received by Ohio Dominican University from the Lilly Foundation. The objective of the grant is for Ohio Dominican University to engage in curriculum development that will promote more inclusion of African American perspectives. One of the means for meeting this objective is through mentor-mentee relationships that team non-African American faculty (mentees) with eminent African American faculty (mentors). This article describes one such mentor-mentee relationship between Dates (mentor) and Schnell (mentee).

Howard University, where Dates is a faculty member and administrator, is a historically Black institution located in Washington, D.C. It is frequently acknowledged as being the leading institution of higher education among other historically Black colleges and universities. Ohio Dominican University, where Schnell is a faculty member, is predominantly White but does have a significant multicultural composition. Roughly 14 percent of Ohio Dominican students are African American and about 10 percent are international students. Ohio Dominican is owned by the Dominican sisters of the Catholic church and has an enrollment of over 2,200 students.

Little has been written about models for curriculum development dealing specifically with communication arts but there are reports on the subject of curriculum development and multicultural inclusiveness. In a *Feedback* article, Dates argues that mass media courses can augment their historical examples by using supplementary textbooks and materials (1991). Much has been written on curriculum development and multicultural inclusiveness that can be applied in communication studies and other disciplines within the social sciences. Helle Bering-Jensen (1990) recommends inclusion of minority contributions in classroom content as a means of supplementing Eurocentric perspectives.

Beverly Tatum (1992) offers strategies for overcoming student resistance to race related content. Emphasis on inclusion of culturally diverse works of literature is described in Pfordresher (1992) and Post (1992). Michael Harris (1992) suggests one means of addressing racial problems is to promote inclusion of African and African American content in U.S. public schools. Kerry Feldman (1992) emphasizes how anthropology departments can be helpful in choosing multicultural education components. Jerry Gaff (1992) claims that multiculturalism has won the war against Eurocentrism and that we should move to the next step of creating inclusive programs that are educationally valuable.

Since the early 1970s many colleges and universities have tried to include minorities in their curriculums through the creation of African American studies departments that stress Black contributions. It is a central premise of the Lilly Foundation grant proposal that "If majority students are to gain the benefits of the minority perspectives, we believe that the contributions of minorities should claim their proper place throughout the curriculum and not be relegated to a 'separate but distinct' area" (Ohio Dominican University, 1991, 13).

The grant proposal speculates on why minority contributions are not included in the American curriculum foundation. "The primary reason, however, appears to be that our present faculty were not exposed to minority contributions in their graduate school training. If a graduate student is not exposed to minority contributions in his or her field in graduate school, the result is that he or she will continue the cycle. Consequently, many of the contributions of minorities have been 'lost' or relegated to nonmainstream areas of study" (Ohio Dominican University, 1991, 13-14).

The aforementioned mentor-mentee relationship was established to begin the long process of change in the communication arts curriculum at Ohio Dominican University. Instant meaningful curriculum change is not easily achieved. Meaningful curriculum change should arise from the faculty rather than from the administration in higher education. Primary goals of this relationship are to: 1) review current courses to determine where important Black contributions may be added, and 2) rework course syllabi to reflect the contributions of African Americans to the discipline. "This approach to curriculum change . . . makes the faculty member a key player in the review and revision of the curriculum. As the curriculum evolves, the faculty will have ownership of that curriculum" (Ohio Dominican University, 1991, 15).

The grant was designed to cover a three-year period between 1992-1995.

> During the grant period, the Black mentors will be on campus at least once a semester and be available to the faculty mentee and to other faculty/administrators and students. In addition to the contributions this program will make to the curriculum, the presence on campus of these Black scholars will greatly enhance the intellectual life and integrity of the campus climate. The Ohio Dominican University mentees will visit their mentors campus to experience a different learning environment and to confer extensively with their mentors. (Ohio Dominican University, 1991, 15)

Thus, curricular change occurred gradually during this three-year period.

The study of communication processes within high-technology and low-technology orientations is continually evolving. The communication arts discipline covers a wide range of subject areas including public speaking, interpersonal communication, organizational communication, mass media, rhetoric, journalism, public relations, broadcasting, theater, and cross-cultural studies. The model described in this article matches Janette Dates, whose specialization is mass media, with Jim Schnell, whose specialty is cross-cultural communication. Although they specialize in different areas within communication arts there is enough common ground between them in communication arts for him to learn from her perspective (i.e., he teaches a course on Mass Media in America although it is not his primary area).

They have focused on five courses Schnell teaches: Rhetorical Communication Theory, Mass Media in America, Persuasion, Communication in the Organization, and a Unity in Diversity course. Examples of course modifications will be described to exemplify how curricular change in communication arts can be implemented.

Rhetorical Communication Theory is an upper-level course at Ohio Dominican University. The course traces the development of rhetoric from the classical period to the British period to the contemporary period. Two primary assignments in the course are a research paper on significant rhetoricians and an oral presentation in class about the rhetorician researched. The suggested list of rhetoricians includes names such as Aristotle, Kenneth Burke, Marie Nichols, Stephen Toulmin, Cicero, David Hume, and Immanuel Kant. No African Americans are included in the list. As a result, the following African American names have been added to the list as possible scholar/rhetoricians (of the African American experience) to be studied: W.E.B. DuBois, Richard Wright, James Baldwin, Martin Luther King Jr., Ralph Ellison, Cornel West, and Toni Morrison. Thus, the list is more inclusive of Afrocentric perspectives.

The Mass Media in America course uses a textbook entitled *Introduction to Mass Media* (Black and Bryant, 1992). This text does a superior job of explaining basic elements of mass media theory but is not perceived to be as inclusive of racially and culturally diverse populations as it could be. Thus, *Introduction to Mass Media* can be supplemented with *Split Image* (Dates and Barlow, 1990) and *Mass Media in America* (Pember, 1992). These works better highlight the participation of African Americans and other historically underrepresented groups in mass media industries. Other sources regarding the role of African Americans are found in an extensive bibliography entitled "Blacks in the Media: Communications Research Since 1978" (Williams, 1990), published by the Howard University Center for Communications Research.

The Persuasion course describes persuasion theory and contemporary applications of persuasion theory. One of these applications involves persuasion in public speaking. Contemporary public speakers can be used for case study analysis in the course. This is an excellent opportunity to naturally include African Americans (i.e., speeches by Martin Luther King Jr. and the Jesse Jackson address at the 1988 Democratic National Convention).

The Communication in the Organization course emphasizes communication in interpersonal, group, and organizational settings. It is suggested that one simple supplementary guideline for text selection in such a course is to analyze possible textbooks for favorable inclusion of traditionally underrepresented racial and cultural groups in case studies, examples, photographs and overall content. This supplementary guideline would obviously be beneficial when considering textbooks for other courses in the communication studies curriculum as well.

The Lilly Foundation grant described earlier in this chapter provided support for development of The Unity in Diversity course. It is a team-taught course. Imali Abala (a Black female) and Jim Schnell (a White male) work together as co-instructors. It is an introductory course that explores the implications of belonging to a culturally pluralistic society with all of its richness, complexities, challenges, and responsibilities. A primary mission of the course is to enhance the ability of the Ohio Dominican diverse student body to interact with culturally diverse individuals who comprise American society.

There is no textbook for the course. Instead, a readings booklet (comprised of many different articles from a variety of sources) has been compiled. Jan Dates has reviewed this readings booklet, and other course materials, and offered feedback regarding how Abala and Schnell can effectively meet course objectives. Unity in Diversity is an experimental course at the time of this writing. It has the potential for being added to the core requirement courses required for all students.

Each mentor-mentee relationship is going to be unique. Thus, it is difficult to dictate specific outcomes that should be achieved in such a relationship. However, Dates and Schnell have found collaboration of communication studies faculty members from a historically Black institution and a historically White institution to yield results that are tangible and less tangible. The tangible results regarding curricular development have been noted. Less tangible results have been realized via the experience of consistent interaction with a colleague from another institution and being able to visit each others campuses. This type of exposure helps to establish a foundation for future curricular development.

Consistent interaction between the professors occurs via the postal service, telephone (conversation and voice mailbox), e-mail, and fax machines. Ideas and feedback have been easily transmitted through these channels. Obviously the face-to-face interaction has been the most meaningful form of communication.

Schnell and Dates visit each other's campuses as part of the Lilly grant program. Dates' visits to Ohio Dominican enhance her understanding of the academic and social climate that exists. Schnell's visits to Howard University provide him with an enriched learning opportunity regarding African American perspectives and the African American experience in America. His visits to Howard include sitting in on classes taught by Dates and others, and time to study in the Moorland-Spingarn Research Center. The Moorland-Spingarn Center is one of the largest collections of African and African American literature in the world. The Center has been especially beneficial in helping Schnell obtain a context for understanding African American academic contributions to higher education.

The spirit of working together, from different cultural perspectives, toward a common ground composed of both perspectives is evidenced in these less tangible areas. It is from within this spirit that toleration of that which is different grows into embracing that which enhances understanding of the familiar. A modified framework for interpreting unfamiliar views benefits not only curricular development, but also the larger issue of working together in other areas of institutional functioning.

Future curricular development can promote an increased inclusion of other perspectives such as Asian, Latino, Arab, and Native American perspectives. Such inclusion is a fundamental premise of this report.

Implementation of this model with other communication studies programs and other academic disciplines is a logistically sound proposition. There will obviously be unique circumstances in any faculty collaboration but the basic framework offered by Schnell and Dates is a model that can be used as a guide for use by other institutions.

Notes

Bering-Jensen, Helle. "Teaching All Things to All People," *Insight*, Vol. 6, Issue 14 (April 2, 1990), 49-51.

Black, Jay and Bryant, Jennings. *Introduction to Mass Communication*. Dubuque, IA: Wm. C. Brown, 1992.

Dates, Jannette. "Multiculturalism and the Broadcast Curriculum: Why Understanding the Issue of Inclusivity is Important to Broadcast Educators," *Feedback*, Fall, 1991, 12-16.

Dates, Jannette and Barlow, William. *Split Image: African Americans in the Mass Media*. Washington, D.C.: Howard University Press, 1990.

Feldman, Kerry D. "Multicultural Education and Anthropology: 'The Rise of Civilization' as a Foundation Course," *Human Organization*, Vol. 51, Issue 2 (Summer, 1992), 185-186.

Gaff, Jerry G. "Beyond Politics," *Change*, Vol. 24, Issue 1 (January 1992), 30-35.

Gordon, Edmund W. and Bhattacharyya, Maitrayee. "Human Diversity, Cultural Hegemony, and the Integrity of the Academic Canon," *Journal of Negro Education*, Vol. 61, Issue 3 (Summer, 1992), 405-418.

Harris, Michael D. "Afrocentrism and Curriculum: Concepts, Issues, and Prospects," *Journal of Negro Education*, Vol. 61, Issue 3 (Summer, 1992), 301-316.

Ohio Dominican University. "Improving Multicultural Climate at a Four-Year University," (1991). A grant proposal funded by the Lilly Foundation.

Pember, Donald. *Mass Media in America*. New York: MacMillan Publishing Co., 1992.

Pfordresher, John. "Better and Different Literature in Our Time," *Design for Arts in Education*, Vol. 93, Issue 4 (March 1992), 2-10.

Post, David. "Through Joshua Gap: Curricular Control and the Constructed Community," *Teachers College Record*, Vol. 93, Issue 4 (Summer, 1992), 673-696.

Tatum, Beverly Daniel. "Talking About Race, Learning About Racism: The Application of Racial Identity Development Theory in the Classroom," *Harvard Educational Review*, Vol. 62, Issue 1 (February 1992), 1-24.

Taylor, Orlando L. "People of Color and the Mass Media: An Unfinished Agenda," *Black Issues in Higher Education*, June 6, 1991, 80.

Viadero, Debra. "Issue of Multiculturalism Dominates Standards Debate," *Education Week*, Vol. 11, Issue 31 (April 22, 1992), 18.

Williams, Michael A. *Blacks and the Media: Communication Research Since 1978*. Washington, D.C.: Howard University, 1990.

Section Three

CASE STUDIES IN
APPLIED SETTINGS

Chapter Eleven

The Hospital Chaplain, Health Care Team, and the Need for Patient Representation in the Health Care Process

Effective communication among medical personnel and patients is fundamental to the achievement of successful health care delivery. This premise has perpetuated significant research in the area of physician-patient interaction (Street and Wiemann, 1986, 1). This chapter addresses the practice of chaplain intervention on behalf of the patient in primary care in an effort to enhance physician-patient interaction and a variety of areas that are directly related to such intentions. Areas to be discussed include the hospital culture, patient functioning within the hospital culture, the communicative role of the hospital chaplain in aiding patients, and contrasting this role against his or her participation as a member of the health care team.

Culture in the communicative context is a summation of ways of living, organizing, and communing built up in a group of human beings and transmitted to newcomers by means of verbal and nonverbal communication. An organization's culture is comprised of elements such as shared norms, rites, rituals, and stories that provide the members with a unique symbolic common ground. Health care institutions exemplify such organizational cultures.

Knapp has reviewed an extensive amount of research that indicates the physical context within which communication occurs can have a negative effect on perceived meanings (Knapp, 1978). For example, when patients enter huge structures, commonly referred to as medical centers, intimidation can begin before they even meet a health professional. This intimidation can be perpetuated by the internal environment which frequently includes mazelike hallways, desks used as barriers, paging systems, medical equipment, and an extensive use of antiseptic white. Similar effects of the physical environment on human interaction have been noted by other researchers (Baum and Valins, 1973, 211-212; Freedman, 1971, 58-61; Haney and Zimbardo, 1975, 2, 29; Stokols, 1976, 8, 49-85).

Aside from the physical environment, physician interpersonal involvement, expressiveness, and dominance can directly affect patient satisfaction and understanding (Street and Wiemann, 1986, 1). While the content dimensions of interactions are central to outcomes of medical interviews, perceptions of relational qualities of these interactions are often more predictive of whether patients are satisfied with their health care and comply with physician recommendations (Ben-Sira, 1976, 3-11; Ben-Sira, 1980, 170-180). For example, Buller reports that the physicians' communicative dominance is negatively related to the patients' satisfaction (Buller, 1985).

Physician dominance, within physician-patient interaction, is frequently noted within the literature (Beisecker, 1986). Mathews found that patients receive clues during interactions which inform them their questions are not welcome (Mathews, 1983, 1371-1378). Mishler contends physician efforts to control discourse has the effect of absorbing and dissolving the patient's self-understanding of his or her problems into the framework of technical medicine (Mishler, 1984). However, it should be noted passive and inactive physicians also elicit negative reactions from patients (Davis, 1968, 274-288). Overall, patients may seek more egalitarian interactions with physicians with both parties committed to contributing and responding (Street and Wiemann, 1986, 21).

In 1972, the American Hospital Association developed a Patient's Bill of Rights. These rights were intended to "contribute to more effective patient care and greater satisfaction for the patient, his or her physician, and the hospital organization" (Becker, 1985, 115). The Patient's Bill of Rights outlines eleven rights that are affirmed. Four of these rights deal specifically with interaction between the patient and his or her physician. These four rights are summarized as follows:

#TWO—The patient has the right to obtain from his or her physician complete current information concerning his or her diagnosis, treatment, and prognosis in terms the patient can be reasonably expected to understand.
#THREE—The patient has the right to receive from his or her physician information necessary to give informed consent prior to the start of any procedures and/or treatment. Except in emergencies, such information for informed consent should include, but not necessarily be limited to, the specific procedure and/or treatment, the medically significant risks involved, and the probable duration of incapacitation.
#FOUR—The patient has the right to refuse treatment to the extent permitted by law, and to be informed of the medical consequences of his or her action.
#TEN—The patient has the right to expect reasonable continuity of care. He or she has the right to know in advance what appointment times and physicians are available and where. (Becker, 1985, 115-118)

There is an increased patient awareness of the Patient's Bill of Rights, but a frequent reluctance of the patient in asserting themselves to make inquiries of their physicians.

A primary approach for chaplains in dealing with patients is to serve as a listener (Becker, 1985, 32-52; Cabot and Dicks, 1936, 189-203; Clebsch and

Jaekle, 1964, 53-54; Clineball, 1984, 205-206). As a listener, the chaplain can become acutely aware of areas of hospital care that the patient does not understand or objects to. Practitioners have acknowledged the practice of serving as an intermediary between patient and physician in such situations. The practice of chaplains serving as intermediaries between patients and physicians was described by Reverend Herman Knodt, Director of Pastoral Care at Grant Hospital in Columbus, Ohio.

Knodt explains that sometimes patients will complain to the chaplain but will be less likely to complain to the physician. An example, in such a situation, would be that the patient is too worn out to have too many tests run in a given period. Since the chaplain exercises extensive listening skills, he or she is more likely to be aware of such complaints than the physician. In such situations, the chaplain might talk with the physician on behalf of the patient, depending on the relationship between the chaplain and the physician.

Before exploring the relationship between the chaplain and the physician it is necessary to acknowledge the existence of mediating factors which make each patient unique. For example, the patient's anxiety about his or her medical condition can affect his or her preference regarding physician interpersonal involvement, expressiveness, and dominance. "Specifically, patients experiencing high anxiety express greater satisfaction with more involved, expressive, and dominant doctors and lower satisfaction with less involved, expressive, and dominant practitioners than do patients experiencing low anxiety" (Street and Wiemann, 1986, 21).

Regardless of the mediating factors, chaplain intervention on behalf of the patient can affect the physician-chaplain relationship. For instance, chaplains have been accused by physicians of being overly optimistic regarding possibilities for the person being helped. Likewise, chaplains may often feel physicians are frequently pessimistic. Different judgments, in these cases, can be understandably based on differences in training, background, and the ways in which professional goals are defined (Wise, 1951, 104-105). For instance, Lutheran health care literature states "In Christ's historical ministry, the healing of the soul and the curing of the body were irrevocably linked" (Wagner, 1974, 103). It is unrealistic to believe all health care providers subscribe to such a belief.

The sick patient is viewed from a number of perspectives. Physicians frequently view patients from a scientific perspective and ministers often view patients from a more philosophical or theological perspective. Granger Westberg, in his book *Minister and Doctor Meet*, explains "Whenever they try to converse they find communication difficult because each looks at the patient's problem from his or her own perspective" (Westberg, 1961, ix).

The faith of the health care provider, chaplain, or physician, can make a difference with some patients on treatment outcomes. "But even here the pastor must be careful that his or her faith is grounded in an understanding of realities, rather than in hopeful, but blind wishing" (Wise, 1951, 105).

As a foundation for further discussion it is necessary to clarify the formation of health care providers working as a team. Health care teams have evolved over the past forty years. Three factors led to their development: 1) medicine has become more specialized and there is a need for specialists to work collectively as a team; 2) the technology of medicine has become much more complicated and there is a need to integrate the talents of varied specialists to use this complicated technology; and 3) an increasing concern with the whole patient. That is, medical problems cannot be understood without looking at the patient as a person (Thompson, 1986, 24).

It is essential for members of an interdisciplinary health care team to work together. But the potential for misunderstandings are usually greater among professionals rather than within professions, as individuals are not always aware of competencies and roles of team members from other professions. Overlapping roles, status differences, and conflicting viewpoints can easily lead to interprofessional conflict (Ducanis and Golin, 1979, 31). Thus, "Conflict and misperceptions among professionals can seriously interfere with collaborative efforts" (Banta and Fox, 1972, 697-722).

Haselkorn cites three primary barriers to communication among professionals: 1) professional ethnocentrism, 2) differences in professional status, and 3) a lack of understanding of other professions (Haselkorn, 1958, 396-400). The effectiveness of a health care team can depend on how well it deals with these areas. This effectiveness will be based on actions that are reactions to interprofessional perceptions.

Rubin and Beckhard stress the importance of expectations about the behavior of other team members. "Each person, in effect, has a set of expectations of how each of the other members should behave as the group works to achieve its goals" (Rubin and Beckhard, 1972, 317-335). As these expectations are monitored against perceptions, conflicting viewpoints can understandably arise as the perception process is relative. For instance, Horwitz states the professional develops four images in his or her interaction with team members: 1) a personal and professional self-image; 2) expectations of his or her own profession in that setting; 3) an understanding of the skills and responsibilities of his or her colleagues; and 4) a perception of his or her colleagues' image of him or her (Horwitz, 1969, 36-39).

Steps have been taken by both pastors and physicians to decrease the perceptual distances that can exist between these two professions. In a study entitled "Cooperation Between Clergy and Family Practice Physicians: A New Area of Ministry," Robert Wikart describes a program which promoted a referral system between physicians and pastors. The program was based primarily on a series of breakfast meetings. His study indicates that familiarity, promoted through these meetings, facilitated the referral system (Weikart, 1986, 156).

Another example is detailed in an article entitled "Pastoral Care of the Sick: A Clinical Course for Medical Students." This course was designed to address the dangers of the so-called "premed" syndrome, which is described as being a situation whereby certain types of individuals are consistently drawn into the medical sciences. The problem being that most premed students receive little formal training in humanistic disciplines. Thus, the course (designed for medical students) deals with "discussion of religious issues and training in recognizing and responding to the spiritual situation of patients" (Sevensky, Ebersole, and Derrickson, 1985, 229).

In conclusion, the aforementioned efforts to improve physician-chaplain interaction seem to be based on a desired familiarity among the various members of the health care team. Using such familiarity as a base, health care team members can better work together to deliver effective health care. In the case of this chapter, such effectiveness has been addressed via chaplain intervention on behalf of the patient. As the influences of interprofessional familiarity are better understood, such familiarity can be more productively stressed within the health care team.

Notes

Banta, H.D. and Fox, R.C. "Role Strains of a Health Care Team in a Poverty Community," *Social Science and Medicine*, 6 (1972), 697-722.

Baum, A. and Valins, S. "Residential Environments, Group Size, and Crowding," *Proceedings of the American Psychological Association,* 1973.

Becker, A.H. *The Compassionate Visitor*. Minneapolis, MN: Augsburg Publishing, 1985.

Beisecker, A.E. "Taking Charge: Attempts to Control the Doctor-Patient Interaction." Paper presented at the Second James Madison University Medical Communication Conference, Harrisonburg, VA, 1986.

Ben-Sira, Z. "The Function of the Professional's Affective Behavior on the Collection of Data," *Journal of Health and Social Behavior*, 17 (1976), 3-11.

Ben-Sira, Z. "Affective and Instrumental Components of the Physician-Patient Relationship: An Additional Dimension of Interaction Theory," *Journal of Health and* Social Behavior, 21 (1980), 170-180.

Buller, M.K. "Physician Communication Style and Health Care Satisfaction." Unpublished M.A. Thesis, Texas Tech University (1985).

Cabot, R.C. and Dicks, R.L. *The Art of Ministering to the Sick*. New York: MacMillan, 1936.

Clebsch, W.A. and Jaekle, C.R. *Pastoral Care in Historical Perspective*. Englewood Cliffs, NJ: Prentice-Hall, 1964.

Clinebell, H. *Basic Types of Pastoral Care and Counseling*. Nashville, TN: Abingdon Press, 1984.

Davis, M. "Variations in Patients' Compliance with Doctors' Advice: An Empirical Analysis of Patterns of Interaction," *American Journal of Public Health*, 58 (1968), 274-288.

Ducanis, A.J. and Golin, A.K. *The Interdisciplinary Health Care Team*. Germantown, MD: Aspen Systems, 1979.

Freedman, J.L. "The Crowd, Maybe Not So Maddening After All," *Psychology Today*, 1971, 58-61, 86.

Haney, C. and Zimbardo, P.G. "It's Tough to Tell a High School from a Prison," *Psychology Today*, 1975, 2, 29.

Haselkorn, F. "Some Dynamic Aspects of Interpersonal Practice in Rehabilitation," *Social Casework*, 39 (1958), 396-400.

Horwitz, J. "Dimensions of Rehabilitation Teamwork," *Rehabilitation Record*, 10 (1969) 36-39.

Knapp, M.L. *Nonverbal Communication in Human Interaction*. New York: Holt, Rinehart, and Winston, 1978.

Mathews, J.J. "The Communication Process in Clinical Settings," *Social Science Medicine*, 17 (1983), 1371-1378.

Mishler, E.G. *The Discourse of Medicine*. Norwood, NJ: Ablex Publishers, 1984.

Rubin, I. and Beckhard, R. "Factors Influencing the Effectiveness of Health Teams," *Milbank Memorial Quarterly*, 3 (1972), 317-335.

Sevensky, R.L., Ebersole, M.L., and Derrickson, P. "Pastoral Care of the Sick: A Clinical Course for Medical Students," *The Journal of Pastoral Care*, 3 (1985), 225-234.

Stokols, D. "The Experience of Crowding in Primary and Secondary Environments," *Environment and Behavior* 8 (1976), 49-85.

Street, R.L. and Wiemann, J.M. "Patient Satisfaction with Physicians' Interpersonal Involvement, Expressiveness, and Dominance." Paper presented at the Communicating with Patients Conference, Tampa, FL, 1986.

Thompson, T.L. *Communication for Health Professionals*. New York: Harper and Row, 1986.

Wagner, J.H. "Mission and Ministry of Congregations in Health Care," in H.C. Letts, ed., *Health Care in America: A National Illness*. Chicago: Lutheran Church in America, 1974.

Weikart, R. "Cooperation Between Clergy and Family Practice Physicians: A New Area of Ministry," *The Journal of Pastoral Care*, 2 (1986).

Westberg, G.E. *Minister and Doctor Meet*. New York: Harper and Brothers, 1961.

Wise, C.A. *Pastoral Care: Its Theory and Practice*. New York: Harper and Brothers, 1951.

Chapter Twelve

The Role of the Hospital Chaplain in Orienting the Patient to the Processes Associated with the Health Care Team

The concept of organizational culture is a viable perspective from which organizations can be studied (Deal and Kennedy, 1982; Pacanowsky and Putnam, 1983; Schwartz and Davis, 1981; Pacanowsky and O'Donnel-Trujillo, 1983; Carbaugh, 1985a). The primary purpose of this chapter is to examine the role of organizational culture as a factor which impacts on patient orientation into the hospital setting. A more extensive analysis will focus on the communicative role of the chaplain in facilitating this orientation process. The information presented will underscore the complementary role the chaplain plays in helping the health care team work toward effective communication in primary care.

Organizational culture is defined as "the unique sense of the place that organizations generate through ways of doing and ways of communicating about the organization. Organizational culture reflects the shared realities in the organization and how these realities create and shape organizational events" (Shockley-Zalabak, 1988, 65). Similar definitions and paralleled applications are provided by a variety of theorists (Harris, 1985, 5; Pacanowsky and O'Donnel-Trujillo, 1982, 122). Furthermore, "the cultural analysts' immediate chore is to discover and interpret the spoken systems that are used in organizations' particular socio-cultural context" (Carbaugh, 1985b, 1). This process of discovery and interpretation relies upon a well-defined frame of reference as a foundation for inquiry.

The communicative elements of culture stress ways of living, organizing and interacting that evolve in groups of people and are passed on to those who are new to the group via varied forms for verbal and nonverbal communication. Such elements include shared norms, rites, rituals, and stories that provide the group members with a unique symbolic common ground. All kinds of organizations, including health care institutions, have such cultures. These cultures, as parallels of national cultures, consistently stress and reaffirm ways of doing and being.

The health care facility can significantly impact interactions among health care consumers and health care providers because the physical context in which the communication occurs has an impact on perceived meanings (Ray and Ray, 1988; Arnold, 1989; Knapp, 1978). This impact occurs because of effects on expectations that result in inhibited exchanges.

Such effects, in the form of intimidation for example, can begin when the health care consumer first enters the health care environment. Hospitals are typically huge structures that have unique variables that affect perception of the environment. Such variables include mazelike hallways, desks used as barriers, paging systems, medical equipment, and an extensive use of antiseptic white. Barriers to understanding can become more problematic when health professionals become so familiar with the physical setting that they do not notice its effect on their interaction with patients (Klinzing and Klinzing, 1985, 26). Similar effects of the physical environment on human interaction have been recognized (Baum and Valins, 1973; Freedman, 1971; Haney and Zimbardo, 1975; Stokols, 1976). The key issue here is that entering a new environment that is foreign to us can serve to detract from our comfort level.

In a more formal sense, the organizational structure of health care institutions is usually hierarchical. Authority and responsibility rest at the top and descend through subordinate levels. Also, specific functions are maintained by components in the structure such as departments and positions, while formal communication networks unite the various elements (Klinzing and Klinzing, 1985).

These informal and formal organizational perspectives help to describe the organizational culture of each health care institution. Additionally, there are other unique characteristics that affect communication within health organizations. These include urgency of activities, status differences, educational differences, and gender socialization differences (Thompson, 1986, 14-15). Regardless of his or her background, each patient must learn to adapt to the particular health care institution culture and understand his or her role within the functioning of the organization.

Although research indicates the need for patient orientation programs (Sharf and Poirier, 1988, 225) usually there is very little formal orientation for the patient. "A primary objective of health education programs is to increase the individual's acceptance and responsibility for his or her own state of health" (Hicks, Spurgeon, and Stubbington, 1988, 15). "Certain general positions have emerged in the literature regarding the contributory role of psychosocial factors to . . . rehabilitation" (Colonese, Fontana, Kerns, and Rosenberg, 1989, 175-176). Thus, it is surprising health care practice has not been affected by health care research regarding implementation of formal orientation programs.

Patient orientation should occur when the patient first enters the health care setting. This is helpful as the patient will be less likely to have misconceptions about what will be happening. The concern with timing is an important communication variable in health education (Kreps, 1988). Ideally, a formal orientation session to instruct and clarify misunderstandings would be helpful. In practice, this function is usually informally handled by various members of the health care team, including the hospital chaplain. Patient orientation, be it positive or negative, occurs the same way first impressions are created in interpersonal communication. If information is not provided to inform the patient, he or she will seek answers to questions (correct or incorrect) to better understand his or her health care experience.

Before addressing the chaplain's role in this orientation process, it will be helpful to clarify the existence of health care teams and the function of the chaplain as a member of the health care team. Health care teams have evolved over the past forty years. Three factors led to their development: 1) medicine has become more specialized and there is a need for specialists to work collectively as a team; 2) the technology of medicine has become much more complicated and there is a need to integrate the talents of varied specialists to use this complicated technology; and 3) an increasing concern with the whole patient (including the spiritual life of the patient). That is, medical problems cannot be understood without looking at the patient as a person (Thompson, 1986, 24).

In the *Psychology of Pastoral Care*, Paul Johnson addresses the third factor.

> The wise physician knows that health is an inner harmony of many vitalities not to be attained by materia medica alone, but rather by restoring the whole personality to well-functioning relationships. . . . As a member of the health care team, the chaplain offers his spiritual ministration. . . . The chaplain has specifically a psychological role to perform; he works not with medical tools but with spiritual instruments that operate in the cure of souls. (Johnson, 1952, 204-205)

Hospital chaplains clearly acknowledge their objective is to work with the mind and soul rather than with curing physical problems. James P. Arnold, Director of Pastoral Care at All Children's Hospital (St. Petersburg, Florida), relates "The chaplain is not there to remove suffering so much as to help people find its deeper meaning for their lives. This is done, in part, by reassuring the sufferer that the struggle is worth it, that meaning is ultimately to be found because God has deemed the sufferer to be meaningful" (Arnold, 1986, 2). With such an objective, the communicative role of the chaplain is not only emphasized, it is essential.

The communicative role of the hospital chaplain is most frequently acknowledged in the area of pastoral counseling. Howard Clinebell, in *Basic Types of Pastoral Care and Counseling*, describes a variety of models, approaches, and concerns within pastoral counseling (Clinebell, 1984). The expression of caring feelings is of primary importance throughout the pastoral counseling processes. "Caring feelings are essential in providing for the emotional needs of patients. Through communication, caring feelings are translated into caring behavior" (Klinzing and Klinzing, 1985, 7). Aday and Anderson and Doyle and Ware have conducted empirical research showing that displays of caring and warmth by health care team members can increase patient satisfaction (Aday and Anderson, 1975; Doyle and Ware, 1977). However, the desire to help can lead to burnout if the health care professional becomes consistently over involved (Miller, Stiff and Ellis, 1988).

It is important for expressions of caring to be offered in language that is understood by the patient. Herman K. Knodt, Director of Pastoral Care at Grant Hospital (Columbus, Ohio), emphasizes the chaplain should speak the "patient's language." That is, the chaplain needs to gauge the level of understanding that the patient is capable of and converse with the patient in a manner that is easily understood by the patient. One idea can be expressed at a variety of language levels.

After achieving a level of understanding, the chaplain's communicative role involves a ministry of dialogue. "It is a ministry of conversation, of the mutual exchange of ideas and feelings, both verbally and nonverbally. . . . All professions in the hospital engage in dialogue with patients. But it is done in concert with other services and activities. Dialogue is the primary service and activity of chaplains. If not done with sensitivity and skill, it leaves the chaplain with little else to offer" (Arnold, 1986, 1).

As a chaplain comes to understand his or her communicative role, as a member of the health care team, these skills can be applied to enhance the patient orientation process. The communicative role of the chaplain within the patient orientation process draws considerably on the chaplain's listening skills. Listening skills are a primary factor in enabling the chaplain to empathize with the patient's situation (Becker, 1985, 33; Clebsch and Jaekle, 1964, 53; Klinzing and Klinzing, 1985, 45). Unfortunately, listening is a communication behavior that seems to be taken for granted (Spearritt, 1962).

As a listener, it is important for the chaplain to respond to feelings expressed, rather than to the intellectual content of patient messages. This can be difficult, as ministerial training emphasizes the intellectualization of beliefs and the importance of finding the "truth" in terms of intellectually formulated propositions (Wise, 1951, 71). Thus, the chaplain must be aware of the dynamics that can enhance understanding of the patient's perceptions.

In aiding the patient orientation process, the chaplain listens to patient feelings about the hospital environment and policies. Based on what is understood, he or she can be instrumental in minimizing patient anxiety by providing additional information and guidance regarding what will be happening during the patient's visit. For instance, Herman Knodt offers the example: "they'll get you up at 7:30 a.m., you will take a shower, they will give you an injection, and about a half hour later roll you down a long hallway. I will be with you when they take you from your room."

In situations where the patient does not fully understand medical procedures the chaplain can request the appropriate health care team member to clarify the area(s) in question for the patient. The assertion that the offering of information improves patient compliance has been confirmed by Francis, Korsch, and Morris (1969) and Freemon, Negrete, Davis, and Korsch (1971).

It should also be noted, in addition to the previous discussion of caring behavior, empirical studies indicate the expression of caring feelings also improves patient compliance with treatment. This finding was substantiated by Becker, Drachman, and Kirscht (1972) and Caplan and Sussman (1966). Thus, the chaplain would be well advised to communicate enough information to meet patient needs, and do so in a caring manner. The same would hold true for other health care team members as well. "Only since the late 1960s, with the growth of new medical schools and the initiation of postgraduate residencies emphasizing primary care, did instruction in communication—typically offered under such labels as 'clinical interviewing,' 'interpersonal skills,' 'introduction to clinical medicine,' or even 'behavioral science'—formally become part of medical education" (Sharf and Poirier, 1988, 225).

The main purpose of this chapter has been to acknowledge the role of organizational culture as a consideration during the process of patient orientation into the hospital setting. The information presented has underscored the complementary communicative role played by the hospital chaplain in helping the health care team to work towards effective communication during this process within primary care.

The study of health care institution cultures is useful as it highlights the elements that define the organization. When the influence of these elements is understood, awareness of such effects can enhance patient orientation into the health care institution setting.

Notes

Aday, L.A., and Anderson R.A. *Access to Medical Care*. Ann Arbor, MI: Health Administration Press, 1975.

Arnold, E. *Interpersonal Relationships: Professional Communication Skills for Nurses*. Philadelphia, PA: W.B. Saunders Co., 1989.

Arnold, J.P. "Patient, Family, Staff Communication: A Chaplain's Perspective." Paper presented at the Communicating with Patients Conference, University of South Florida, 1986.

Baum, A. and Valins, S. 1973. "Residential Environments, Group Size, and Crowding," *Proceedings of the American Psychological Association*.

Becker, A.H. *The Compassionate Visitor*. Minneapolis, MN: Augsburg Publishing, 1985.

Becker, M.H. Drachman, R.H., and Kirscht J.P. "Motivations as Predictors of Health Behavior," *Health Services Reports*, 87 (1972), 852-861.

Caplan, E. and Sussman, M. "Rank Order of Important Variables for Patient and Staff Satisfaction," *Journal of Health and Human Behavior*, 7 (1966), 133-138.

Carbaugh, D.B. "Cultural Communication and Organizing," *International and Intercultural Communication Annual*, 9 (1985a), chapter 2.

Carbaugh, D.B. "Cultural Communication as Organization: A Case Study of Speech in an Organizational Setting." Paper presented at the annual meeting of the Speech Communication Association, Denver, CO, 1985b.

Clebsch, W.A. and Jaekle, C.R. *Pastoral Care in Historical Perspective*. Englewood Cliffs, NJ: Prentice-Hall, 1964.

Clinebell, H. *Basic Types of Pastoral Care and Counseling*. Nashville, TN: Abingdon Press, 1984.

Colonese, K.L., Fontana, A.F., Kerns, R.D., and Rosenberg, R.L. "Support, Stress, and Recovery from Coronary Heart Disease: A Longitudinal Causal Model," *Health Psychology*, 8 (1989).

Deal, T.E. and Kennedy A.A. *Corporate Cultures: The Rites and Rituals of Corporate Life*. Reading, MA: Addison-Wesley, 1982.

Doyle, B.J. and Ware, J.E. "Physician Conduct and Other Factors That Affect Consumer Satisfaction With Medical Care," *Journal of Medical Education*, 23 (1977), 283-292.

Francis, V., Korsch, B.M., and Morris, M.J. "Gaps in Doctor-Patient Communication," *New England Journal of Medicine* (1969), Vol. 280, 535-540.

Freedman, J.L. "The Crowd, Maybe Not So Maddening After All," *Psychology Today*, (1971), 58-61, 86.

Freemon, B., Negrete, V., Davis, M., and Korsch, B. "Gaps in Doctor-Patient Communication: Doctor-Patient Interaction Analysis," *Pediatric Research*, 5 (1971), 298-311.

Haney, C. and Zimbardo, P.G. "It's Tough to Tell a High School from a Prison," *Psychology Today*, (1975), 2, 29.

Harris, T. "Characteristics of Organizational Cultures: A Communication Perspective." Paper presented at the annual meeting of the Speech Communication Association, Denver, CO, 1985.

Hicks, C., Spurgeon, P., and Stubbington, J. "The Importance of Psycho-Social Variables in Changing Attitudes and Behavior," *Health Education Journal*, 47 (1988).

Johnson, P.E. *Psychology of Pastoral Care*. Nashville, TN: Abingdon Press, 1952.

Klinzing, D. and Klinzing, D. *Communication for Allied Health Professionals*. Dubuque, IA: Wm. C. Brown, 1985.

Knapp, M.L. *Nonverbal Communication in Human Interaction*. New York: Holt, Rinehart, and Winston, 1978.

Kreps, G. "Communication and Health Education in Health Care Delivery." Paper presented at the annual meeting of the Speech Communication Association in New Orleans, LA, 1988.

Miller, K.I., Stiff, J.B., and Ellis, B.H. "Communication and Empathy as Precursors to Burnout Among Human Service Workers," *Communication Monographs*, 55 (1988).

Pacanowsky, M. and Putnam, L.L. *Communication and Organizations: An Interpretive Approach*. Beverly Hills, CA: Sage Publications, 1983.

Pacanowsky, M. and O'Donnel-Trujillo, N. "Communication and Organizational Cultures," *Western Journal of Speech Communication*, 46 (1982).

Pacanowsky, M. and O'Donnel-Trujillo, N. "Organizational Communication as Cultural Performance," *Communication Monographs*, 50 (1983) 127-147.

Ray, G. and Ray, E.B. "Patients Perspectives of Nonverbal Cues in Health Messages." Paper presented at the annual meeting of the Speech Communication Association, New Orleans, LA, 1988.

Schwartz, H. and Davis, S. "Matching Corporate Culture and Business Strategy," *Organizational Dynamics* (Summer, 1981), 30-48.

Sharf, B.F. and Poirier, S. 1988. "Exploring (Un)Common Ground: Communication and Literature in a Health Care Setting," *Communication Education*, 37 (July 1988), 225.

Shockley-Zalabak, P. *Fundamentals of Organizational Communication*. New York: Longman Press, 1988.

Spearritt, D. *Listening Comprehension—A Factual Analysis*. Melbourne, Australia: G.W. Sons, 1962.

Stokols, D. "The Experience of Crowding in Primary and Secondary Environments," *Environment and Behavior* (1976) Issue 8, 49-85.

Thompson, T.L. *Communication for Health Professionals*. New York: Harper and Row, 1986.

Wise, C.A. *Pastoral Care: Its Theory and Practice*. New York: Harper and Brothers, 1951.

Chapter Thirteen

Analyzing C-SPAN in the Classroom to Improve Student Learning

The basic communication course can be a forum for a variety of teaching strategies. Selection of said strategies is determined by variables such as topic, objectives, audience, and context. This chapter describes methodology for studying presentations made by President George Bush during the Persian Gulf War as an example of how public speakers can be studied using the Purdue University Public Affairs Video Archives. Such methodology is beneficial in the classroom and with individual research. The Purdue University Public Affairs (C-SPAN) Video Archives is the primary source used in this study because analysis focuses not only on literal statements but on nonverbal communication channels as well. The teaching and research functions of C-SPAN usage are mutually enriching.

To obtain videotapes, call the Public Affairs Video Archives at Purdue University (800-423-9630) and give them the name of the person being researched. They will provide a free index of all videotapes they have of that person. Each videotape listed will have a brief description of the event. After receiving and reviewing the list, desired tapes can be ordered by calling the Public Affairs Video Archives at the aforementioned phone number. They will provide an order form and answer questions regarding the ordering process. Videotape costs are listed in the index provided by them.

Written transcripts of speeches and presentations by President Bush provide literal meanings but provide no insights regarding nonverbal communication cues. Usage of transcripts (as a singular source) has serious limitations because so much of our meanings are communicated through nonverbal channels. Thus, transcripts convey a limited portion of a speaker's overall meaning. Videotapes of the actual speeches provide verbal statements, nonverbal messages, and situational context. A transcript can describe the situational context but a videotape allows you to see and hear the situational context.

This research uses Persian Gulf War presentations delivered by President Bush between August 2, 1990 (the day Iraq invaded Kuwait), and January 16, 1991 (when the air war against Iraq began). Bush was selected for analysis because, as President, he was a major statesman. The Persian Gulf War time period was selected because it is a definite time period that includes numerous presentations by Bush on a particular subject.

These presentations were ordered, on 1/2 inch VHS tapes, from the Purdue University Public Affairs Video Archives after obtaining the Archives index of C-SPAN tapes dealing with the Persian Gulf War. Every presentation by Bush available from the C-SPAN tape index for the aforementioned period was used in this study. Contexts of delivery include news conferences, speeches, news briefings, and White House events. Using all of the Bush presentation tapes available from the C-SPAN index provides an appropriate way to limit/define the tape sample studied.

The study of the Bush videotaped presentations allows analysis of the President's rhetoric in relation to events and intentions in the Persian Gulf War. Analysis of literal verbal statements provides insights regarding labeling (usage of action verbs) and the use of symbols. This is exemplified by Bush describing the Iraq troop movement into Kuwait as an "invasion" and "unchecked aggression." Analysis of nonverbal communication provides insights regarding the role of vocalics and paralanguage cues (pitch, rate, tone, and volume), occulesics (eye behavior), and kinesics (gesturing). Analysis of the verbal statements and nonverbal messages is enhanced through appreciation of situational contexts the statements and messages are communicated within. For instance, Bush speaking solely to a television audience from the oval office is a different context than when he's addressing a joint session of Congress.

Study of these areas (verbal statements, nonverbal communication, and situational contexts) can be done using the chart provided as appendix #1 to this chapter. This chart uses the Aristotelian perspectives of logos, ethos, and pathos as a framework for interpreting Bush's reasoning, character, and emotional appeal. His reasoning, character, and emotional appeal are conveyed through his verbal statements, nonverbal communication, and situational contexts. Use of this framework benefits students because, if they are not familiar with logos, ethos, and pathos, this approach will orient them to the concepts and their application. If they are familiar with these concepts then this approach will allow them to sharpen that understanding.

The eleven tapes studied in the project can be analyzed using the chart. The chart is appropriate for usage by individual researchers or with students in classroom settings. Review of each tape begins by noting the tape date, title, length, topic, type of presentation, and location of presentation. This information helps define the situational context of the presentation. It is easily obtained from the tape description provided on each cassette (except for the topic, which is best ascertained after viewing the tape).

Ideally, each tape should be viewed three times by students. This allows specific focus on logos, ethos, and pathos. The first viewing is for analysis of logos (use of reasoning). The chart instructs the student to provide a brief summary of main points and describe how these main points are substantiated. The student also responds to the statement "The speaker effectively clarifies main points of the position taken and provides appropriate substantiation for these main points." They can respond strongly agree, agree, neutral, disagree, or strongly disagree.

The second viewing is for analysis of ethos (character of the speaker). The chart instructs the student to provide a brief summary of main factors that comprise the speaker's character (i.e., trustworthiness, expertness, goodwill, and charisma) and how this character is conveyed. The student also responds to the statement "The speaker effectively conveys positive character." They respond strongly agree, agree, neutral, disagree, or strongly disagree.

The third viewing is for analysis of pathos (stimulation of emotions). The chart instructs the student to provide a brief summary of the speaker's stimulation of audience emotions (i.e., anger, friendship, fear, shame, and/or pity) and how this stimulation is achieved. The student also responds to a statement "The speaker effectively stimulates audience emotions." They respond strongly agree, agree, neutral, disagree, or strongly disagree.

Analysis of the presentations using this chart provides a means by which reviewers can formulate concise interpretations. Without such a framework for interpretation reviewers can too easily generalize their observations if they don't have specific phenomena they're watching for. Use of the Likert Scale (strongly agree, agree, neutral, disagree, strongly disagree) in relation to the statements posed for logos, ethos, and pathos provides a foundation for classroom discussion of the presentations (i.e., presentations can be numerically scored regarding speaker effectiveness in these three areas). Such numerical scoring can be done using the 5—strongly agree, 4—agree, 3—neutral, 2—disagree, and 1—strongly disagree values indicated in appendix #1.

An area for additional comments is provided at the bottom of the chart. Occasionally the reviewer may have an observation that does not directly relate to logos, ethos, or pathos that he or she feels is relevant to the process of presentation evaluation. For instance, if the speaker is wearing uncommon clothing for the speaking situation.

The eleven presentations used in this study are listed in the Notes section. I have analyzed each tape using the aforementioned chart. This type of analysis, based on my interpretation, is intended to be a pilot study. A more thorough analysis can obviously be achieved by using the survey with students and quantifying their observations (using the Likert Scale numerical ordering). Thus, consistencies in the data can be used to build findings and conclusions from.

Findings, based on verbal statements, nonverbal communication, and situational contexts, illustrate the benefit of using videotapes of presentations rather than written transcripts, in that nonverbal communication and situational contexts cannot be evaluated using written transcripts. It is my contention that such nonverbal communication and situational contexts impact viewer impression formation.

An example of such a finding is located in the tape titled "Situation in the Persian Gulf" (1990). Review of the tape indicates Bush consistently pronounces Saddam Hussein in a manner different than journalists, spokespersons, and those interviewed. This unique pronunciation is of the name Saddam. Bush's unique pronunciation of Saddam rhymes with "Adam." The more common pronunciation of Saddam can be described as "Saw-dawm" (with emphasis on the first syllable). The pronunciation of Saddam used by Bush is incorrect and translates to "shoe-shine boy." The more common translation of Saddam is correct and translates to "highly revered one." This usage exemplifies a unique form of (what could be referred to as a) "psychological operation."

A primary finding from the videotape analysis deals with the importance of what type of presentation Bush is making. These types, or contexts, of delivery include news conferences, speeches, news briefings, and White House events. The more control Bush has over the environment, and the more prepared he is with his message, correlates with his ability to convey his desired meaning. For instance, he is most effective in an oval office speech, where he has a prepared text and no live audience to contend with, than he is in a news conference, where he is responding to questions spontaneously. The following excerpts from the author's observations support this finding.

The tape titled "Bush and Thatcher on Invasion of Kuwait" (1990) is a news conference where Bush presents a prepared statement. Review of the videotape indicates Bush's most notable factor, regarding character, is his expert image. His consistency with his position conveys an image of being knowledgeable and informed. The tape titled "U.S.-Persian Gulf Resolutions" (1991), in contrast, is a news conference where Bush presents a prepared statement and responds to questions. In such a situation he has less control of himself and the behavior of others, as manifested in the questions asked and the aggressiveness with which they are asked. Review of the videotape indicates Bush appeared to be mildly disheveled (i.e., his hair was greasy and uncombed). This implies his hands-on approach with the Persian Gulf situation (making his normal well-kept appearance less of a priority).

Bush is most polished and "presidential" in a speech from the White House Oval Office ("Troop Deployment," 1990). Review of the tape finds Bush speaks from the Oval Office (which enhances his credibility) and his family photos provide a backdrop (which enhances his humanitarian appeal). He is almost "fatherly" (when he provides a benevolently animated explanation for U.S. actions). The effect of environment is a factor in "Events in the Persian Gulf" (1990a), that is a Bush news conference from his vacation home in Kennebunkport, Maine. He speaks from his vacation home, outside, and wearing a blue blazer over a sport shirt. He seems well rested, comfortable, well informed (regarding his initial statement), and steadfast. The environment, and his familiarity with it, enhances his credibility.

"Presidential Address on Persian Gulf" (1990) is Bush's speech to a joint session of Congress. This presentation was designed to show a united American front, thus Bush could count on audience support from members of the House and Senate. Bush delivered a well-polished speech. It was clear, concise, and delivered with a good sense of timing. A good example of statesman oratory (effective pauses and moderately animated). His logic was substantiated, his emotional appeals were built upon widely held beliefs of his audience, and his credibility was pronounced given he was the president addressing a joint session of Congress. This speech is a high point regarding Bush's ability to stimulate emotion. His speech was interrupted roughly twenty-four times with applause.

The benefit of videotape analysis, over transcript analysis, is apparent in "Geneva Meeting on Persian Gulf Crisis" (1991). Review of the tape indicates Bush inspires confidence and his leadership role is intact (he is flanked by U.S. and United Nations flags). One gets the feeling there is little posturing. Bush seems genuinely frustrated (especially as conveyed in his tone of voice). Thus, the aforementioned apparent preference for videotape analysis over transcript analysis is illustrated via the backdrop within which he speaks and his resolute tone of voice.

There are inherent weaknesses with the proposed model of analysis (using the aforementioned process whereby students observe each tape three times). Findings will be based on subjective interpretations of the videotaped presentations. When such interpretations differ in the classroom, this can be foundation for classroom discussion regarding why interpretations differ (or why similarities exist when such similarities occur). The subjective nature of this kind of inquiry is readily acknowledged. However, use of a subjective instrument does not negate or affirm the usefulness of the instrument. It merely substantiates that findings must be considered in light of the method used to arrive at the findings. The exemplification of this issue in the classroom can benefit student learning.

Again, study of Bush exemplifies how other public speakers can be analyzed. Findings (and videotape excerpt examples) are appropriate for classroom usage, as described in this paper, and delivery at professional conferences. Student understanding can benefit in a variety of courses in the communication studies curriculum, including mass media, persuasion, cross-cultural communication, rhetorical communication theory, interpersonal communication, and public speaking. For instance, Bush's presentations are conveyed by the mass media, are often persuasive or informative, involve expression of meanings to culturally diverse audiences, and employ rhetorical strategies. Regarding individual research efforts, findings (and methodological considerations) would be relevant for presentation in many of the areas of the National Communication Association's annual national meeting (i.e., Media Forum) and suitable for publication in professional journals.

The goal of this chapter has been to describe methodology for studying presentations made by President George Bush during the Persian Gulf War. The study of Bush exemplifies how other public speakers can be analyzed using the Purdue University Public Affairs Video Archives. The strengths of the methodology described are that the use of videotape provides considerably more context than written transcripts, and videotape can be used effectively in the classroom. A weakness of the methodology described is that individual research findings without surveying viewers and quantifying their responses can be seen as lacking objectivity. As a pilot study this chapter illustrates the strengths and weaknesses of using videotape as a database.

The evolving information age offers teachers a variety of new tools for conveying class material. Examination of such tools as exemplified in this article is based on the belief we should clearly seek to acknowledge strengths and weaknesses of each innovation and work to capitalize on the strengths.

Notes

"Bush and Thatcher on Invasion of Kuwait," *C-SPAN Public Affairs Video Archives.* August 2, 1990 (ID 13394).

"Events in the Persian Gulf," *C-SPAN Public Affairs Video Archives.* August 27, 1990a (ID 13703).

"Events in the Persian Gulf," *C-SPAN Public Affairs Video Archives.* August 28, 1990b (ID 13717).

"Geneva Meeting on Persian Gulf Crisis," *C-SPAN Public Affairs Video Archives.* January 9, 1991 (ID 15641).

"Persian Gulf War: Fitzwater Announcement," *C-SPAN Public Affairs Video Archives.* January 16, 1991 (ID 15762).

"Presidential Address on Persian Gulf," *C-SPAN Public Affairs Video Archives.* September 11, 1990 (ID 13945).

"Presidential Address: Persian Gulf Air War Begins." *C-SPAN Public Affairs Video Archives.* January 16, 1991 (ID 15723).

"Reaction to Iraqi Invasion of Kuwait," *C-SPAN Public Affairs Video Archives.* August 2, 1990 (ID 13395).

"Situation in Persian Gulf," *C-SPAN Public Affairs Video Archives.* August 8, 1990 (ID 13458).

"Troop Deployment," *C-SPAN Public Affairs Video Archives.* August 8, 1990 (ID 13455).

"U.S.-Persian Gulf Resolutions," *C-SPAN Public Affairs Video Archives.* January 12, 1991 (ID 15678).

Appendix #1

Tape Date:	Topic:
Length:	Type of Presentation:
Title:	Location:

SD—strongly disagree   D—disagree   N—neutral
A—agree   SA—strongly agree

LOGOS (use of reasoning)
Provide a brief summary of main points and describe how these main points are substantiated.

The speaker effectively clarifies main points of the position taken and provides appropriate substantiation of these main points.

SD	D	N	A	SA
1	2	3	4	5

ETHOS (character of speaker)
Provide a brief summary of main factors that comprise speaker's character (i.e., trustworthiness, expertness, goodwill, and charisma) and how this character is conveyed.

The speaker effectively conveys positive character (i.e., trustworthiness, expertness, goodwill, and charisma).

SD	D	N	A	SA
1	2	3	4	5

PATHOS (stimulation of emotions)
Provide a brief summary of speaker's stimulation of audience emotions (i.e., anger, friendship, fear, shame, and/or pity) and how this stimulation is achieved.

The speaker effectively stimulates audience emotions (i.e., anger, friendship, fear, shame, and pity).

SD	D	N	A	SA
1	2	3	4	5

Chapter Fourteen

Emphasizing a Multicultural Climate as a Group Dynamic in the Classroom

This chapter seeks to help faculty understand their cross-cultural awareness in the classroom and to provide a means for improvement in this area. This objective is addressed through the use of a self-reporting instrument that faculty can use to gauge their awareness of primary areas of cross-cultural difference in the classroom. I purport sensitivity with cross-cultural differences leads to cross-cultural awareness, which in turn leads to improved cross-cultural understanding.

Approximate Time Required

About one to two hours is required.

Materials Needed

I use a survey entitled "Culture Bound Areas for Personal Reflection." It is based on an outline of culture bound areas that was created by the National Association for Developmental Education. The survey is included at the end of this article in the "Student Handout" section. It includes culture bound areas that can be interpreted and emphasized in different ways depending on the cultural backgrounds of the individuals involved. These culture bound areas can hinder the learning process.

It is a self-reporting instrument. Respondents select a response to each statement in each area: strongly agree, agree, neutral, disagree, and strongly disagree. These are areas that are frequently interpreted and emphasized differently depending on the cultural background of the individual. Sensitivity with these areas offers opportunities to improve classroom interaction. This improvement is based on enhanced understanding.

This can help respondents gauge their cross-cultural awareness by comparing and contrasting their perceptions with others who complete the survey. This instrument focuses on teacher expectations, standards, personal perspectives, approaches in common situations, and how these areas can benefit or detract from the classroom environment. Interpretation of these areas can vary depending on the cultural or subcultural background of the respondent. Such variance of interpretation will be more pronounced among people from cultural backgrounds that are significantly different than if the individuals are from cultural backgrounds more similar in nature.

The areas addressed in the survey deal with issues that can be foundations of misunderstanding among international students and faculty members. For instance, I.F. states "If a student is caught in an academically dishonest action, he or she should be expelled from school." The question of what is academically dishonest is problematic because what is appropriate in one culture can be inappropriate in another culture. For instance, plagiarism in the U.S. culture is a serious offense that can result in expulsion from school. Plagiarism in countries such as China is more commonly practiced since ideas are more freely exchanged without as much concern for referencing sources.

Sensitivity with these issues is helpful when interacting with the wide range of subcultures that compose the varied U.S. culture. Problems of understanding that occur among international cultures parallel misunderstandings among U.S. subcultures. This lack of shared meaning is based on differing frames of reference. The different frames of reference do not necessarily indicate contradictory interpretations of the culture bound areas. More likely they reveal one continuum with varied interpretations along that continuum. These variances will correspond with differences among the cultural backgrounds compared.

Rationale

Concern with the multicultural classroom has increased considerably during the past thirty years. With more and more cultural backgrounds represented in the American classroom it is important faculty consider the cultural variables that are introduced in such a situation. These variables can serve as obstacles or as opportunities in the learning process.

It is my contention cross-cultural misunderstandings that occur among world cultures parallel cross-cultural misunderstandings that occur among American subcultures. Both are grounded in a lack of shared experiences and frames of reference. I propose that sensitivity with cross-cultural differences leads to cross-cultural awareness, which in turn leads to improved cross-cultural understanding.

Cross-cultural awareness in the multicultural classroom has become an important issue in recent years for two main reasons: a continued increase of international students studying in the United States and an increased emphasis on faculty skills for dealing with minorities in the classroom. Regarding the latter, acts of racism have increased significantly on college campuses during recent years and minorities have responded by emphasizing the need for cross-cultural sensitivity in and out of the classroom. Unfortunately, faculty approaches to maintain cultural equilibrium in the classroom can be mistaken for cross-cultural insensitivity.

Culture provides a context for teaching and learning. As such it is the frame of reference for interpreting what we encounter in the classroom. An irony in this situation is that one can experience "culture shock" in his or her own classroom without leaving the home country.

There are typically four stages of culture shock: the honeymoon, crisis, recovery and adjustment stages. It occurs when we experience confusion, anger, or despair as a result of our unsuccessful attempts to deal with cultural practices that are new or foreign to us. This usually happens when we are outside of our own culture but it can happen when dealing with individuals who are culturally different than us in our own culture.

A brief description of the four stages follows. The honeymoon stage occurs during our first interactions with a new culture when we are intrigued with our new surroundings. The crisis stage occurs when we become frustrated with a problem situation we cannot resolve. The recovery stage occurs when we learn how to resolve the issue. The final adjustment stage occurs when the issue is resolved and we have regained a sense of balance.

I have encountered varied types of culture shock scenarios in my teaching. The previously described situation, regarding differing views on academic dishonesty in the United States and China, conveys implications with the culture shock phenomenon. The honeymoon stage was evidenced when I embraced learning new things about the Chinese culture. A crisis stage unfolded when I observed students plagiarizing from outside sources when writing their papers. Recovery was evidenced when I learned degrees of plagiarism are more common in Chinese universities. Adjustment was achieved when I told my students this was against the way I had been trained in the United States but that I would adopt the Chinese approach on the issue during my time in China.

Similarly, I have encountered situations in the United States (when working with culturally different students) that correspond to the scenario I describe from China. The following describes such a situation. Regarding the honeymoon stage, I had two Vietnamese students who were new to the United States. I wanted to get to know them because I am interested in Vietnamese history and they were "boat people" who had escaped from Vietnam. Regarding the crisis stage, their understanding of U.S. culture was minimal and they had great difficulty understanding various assignments in the classroom. Regarding recovery, I modified their assignments, basing them on more universal understandings, so the Vietnamese students could complete the course objectives. Regarding adjustment, we achieved an academic basis for common understanding.

One should consider many variables of interpersonal interaction when involved in cross-cultural encounters. One such variable deals with high-context communication processes and low-context communication processes. In high-context cultures people present messages indirectly and meanings will evolve. Much meaning is communicated through paralanguage cues and gesture. High-context cultures tend to be located in Asia.

People who are from low-context cultures tend to be more direct when presenting messages. Obviously there is much room for confusion and incorrect interpretation of intentions when a person from a low-context culture interacts with a person from a high-context culture. Low-context cultures are mainly European countries and countries with European roots such as the United States.

If people have different perceptions of the culture bound areas this does not necessarily equate with them having different values. They can have similar values but the *expression* of these values that are grounded in cultural communicative norms can differ significantly. Understanding in such cross-cultural encounters can be problematic because differing perceptions of these culture bound areas can reflect differing values *and* differing communication processes. A keen sense of awareness with this dynamic can be helpful. Students from all cultural backgrounds will obviously benefit from a multicultural classroom environment that is sensitive to various cultural and subcultural backgrounds.

Things to Do before Class

Consider the elements and dynamics of the multicultural classroom. It is a myth to believe it is enough to treat culturally (or subculturally) different students like they are from your own culture (or subculture). Such a view is too ethnocentric. A basic goal can be to create a classroom environment that meets culturally different students "halfway." Intentions to establish a clear understanding can serve as a base for clear understanding.

In general terms, awareness of the affective, cognitive, and interpersonal domains of cross-cultural dialog can enhance interaction. The affective domain deals with acceptance of other cultural backgrounds. The cognitive domain stresses understanding of other cultural backgrounds. The interpersonal domain promotes development of communication skills for interacting with individuals from other cultural backgrounds.

What to Do during Class

Faculty members can begin their self-inquiry by tape recording their lectures for personal review. When listening to such tapes, one can listen for use of sarcasm, language norms, vocal animation, supporting statements through repetition, level of vocabulary, pronunciation and rate of speech. These areas can be variables in cross-cultural communication.

Focus on the following survey areas can be revealing:

I.   A. Teacher-student communication should be based on formal (rather than informal) interaction.
II. A. I handle emotionally charged issues and conflict by never losing control of myself or my control over the classroom.
II. B. Humor is essential in the classroom.
III. A. It is important for me to treat students the same. They should never know if I really like them individually or not.

What to Do after the Activity

The taped lectures can be used to evaluate these areas. When doing this it is important to consider how interpretation of the culture bound areas differ in each culture. The individual should reflect on how his or her approach fits within his or her culture/subculture and how his or her approach could differ from other cultural/subcultural orientations.

The awareness that grows from cross-cultural sensitivity, in settings such as the multicultural classroom, can help reduce possible barriers to understanding in ways that help create learning opportunities. We can seek to better understand not just what we teach but how we teach it. Faculty self-evaluation of these considerations is a solid step toward such understanding.

Alternate Uses or Extensions

This survey can also be used with students. They can complete the survey and compare/contrast their answers with one another. Such discussion can promote meaningful dialog regarding the conceptual foundations that support various responses. This can be equally beneficial regardless of whether or not there are consistencies among responses to the survey areas.

Notes

Anderson, Peter A. "Explaining Intercultural Differences in Nonverbal Communication." Paper presented at the annual meeting of the National Communication Association, Boston, MA, November 1987.

Brislin, Richard W. "Cross-Cultural Research in Psychology," *Annual Review of Psychology*, 34 (1983), 363-400.

Geertz, Clifford. *The Interpretation of Cultures*. New York: Basic Books, 1973.

Hall, Edward T. *Beyond Culture*. Garden City, NY: Anchor Books, 1976.

Triandis, Harry C. "Reflections on Trends in Cross-Cultural Research," *Journal of Cross-Cultural Psychology*, 11 (1980), 35-38.

Whorf, Benjamin L. *Language, Thought, and Reality*. New York: John Wiley & Sons, 1956.

Student Handout

SA—strongly agree   A—agree   N—neutral   D—disagree
SD—strongly disagree

CULTURE BOUND AREAS FOR PERSONAL REFLECTION:

I. EXPECTATIONS AND STANDARDS	SA	A	N	D	SD
A. Teacher-student communication should be based on formal (rather than informal) interaction.	5	4	3	2	1
B. Dress and cleanliness is important.	5	4	3	2	1
C. If a student is academically unprepared, it is primarily his or her own fault.	5	4	3	2	1
D. Student should have a lot of free time.	5	4	3	2	1
E. Respect for authority is important.	5	4	3	2	1
F. If a student is caught in an academically dishonest action, he or she should be expelled from school.	5	4	3	2	1

II. APPROACHES	SA	A	N	D	SD
A. I handle emotionally charged issues and conflict by never losing control of myself or my control over the classroom.	5	4	3	2	1
B. Humor is essential in the classroom.	5	4	3	2	1
C. I enjoy some students less than others.	5	4	3	2	1

III. PREFERENCES	SA	A	N	D	SD
A. It is important for me to treat students the same. They should never know if I really like them individually.	5	4	3	2	1

B. I prefer group (instead of individual) learning   5   4   3   2   1
   activities.

C. I prefer docile (instead of aggressive) students.   5   4   3   2   1

"Today we are faced with the preeminent fact that, if civilization is to survive, we must cultivate the science of human relationships—the ability of all peoples, of all kinds, to live together and work together, in the same world, at peace."

Franklin D. Roosevelt
(April 13, 1945)

Chapter Fifteen

Public Speaking Instruction as a Group Experience

This chapter describes a short course for middle-school students, sponsored by the Higher Education Council of Columbus (Ohio), that I developed. I have completed a Ph.D. in speech-communication and am a full professor of communication studies. I earned certification to teach in secondary-level public schools and have worked with middle-school students.

Within the short course, students enhance self-expression capabilities using public speaking as a communicative channel. Students are encouraged to speak on topics they are knowledgeable about and interested in. This allows students to improve self-expression, observe self-expression practices of other students, and learn about new subjects. Three types of speaking are emphasized: Speech of Introduction, Informative Presentation, and Impromptu Speech. This is a skills oriented "hands-on" course. Students receive instruction and perform in accordance with assigned instruction.

The short course is divided into three segments that meet on three consecutive Wednesday evenings. Classes meet from 5:30-9:00 p.m. with a thirty-minute break for dinner. A course description is distributed to middle schools in the Columbus, Ohio, area. The course plans for class meetings are designed to meet the aforementioned objectives. The following descriptions highlight primary aspects of each class meeting.

Class meeting number one includes: 1) introduction to the course, 2) self-introductions by students (sitting in a circle), 3) instructions for the Speech to Inform/How-to-do-it Speech, 4) an example of the Speech to Inform/How-to-do-it Speech delivered by the instructor, and 5) Impromptu Speeches by students (dealing with topics assigned by the instructor).

The Speech to Inform/How-to-do-it Speech is four to five minutes and is videotaped. Students prepare a keyword outline (emphasizing introduction, body, and conclusion) and are to use a visual aid. Students are encouraged to speak on topics they are knowledgeable about or interested in. A volunteer student videotapes the instructor, as he or she delivers an example speech to help familiarize students with the taping process. The tape is replayed in class.

Students are videotaped when they deliver their impromptu speeches. Each speech is two to three minutes. Taped student speeches are replayed for the class. This is followed by a brief discussion to relieve student anxiety about being videotaped.

Remaining class time for the evening is spent on lecture. Lecture topics are intended to help students in the preparation and delivery of their speeches. Lecture topics are described later in this paper.

Class meeting number two includes: 1) student delivery of Speech to Inform/How-to-do-it Speeches (videotaped) followed with brief evaluations by the instructor at the end of each speech, 2) portions of each videotaped speech (about two minutes) are replayed in class, 3) instructions for the Current Events Speech, 4) an example of the Current Events Speech delivered by the instructor.

The brief evaluation by the instructor at the end of each Speech to Inform/How-to-do-it Speech is intended to provide constructive criticism to help students improve on the next speech. Positive aspects are noted along with at least one suggested improvement. Time is also allotted for questions from the audience.

The Current Events Speech is three to four minutes and can be about any current event (local, national, or international) topic. Students are encouraged to seek topics from newspapers and/or magazines. Speeches are to be videotaped. Students prepare a keyword outline (emphasizing introduction, body, and conclusion).

Remaining time for the evening is spent on closing comments regarding the Speech to Inform/How-to-do-it Speech, questions about the Current Events Speech, and lecture. The relevance of lecture topics is highlighted using examples from speeches already delivered by students.

Class meeting number three includes: 1) students deliver Current Events Speeches (videotaped) followed by brief evaluation by the instructor at the end of each speech, 2) portions of each videotaped speech (about two minutes) are replayed in class, 3) Impromptu Speeches are delivered by students, 4) lecture, and 5) certificates of course completion are given to students at the close of the course.

The question period following each Current Events Speech receives greater emphasis than with the Speech to Inform/How-to-do-it Speech. An objective is to enhance student ability to respond to questions and speak spontaneously. Similarly, the Impromptu Speech helps students improve their ability to speak spontaneously.

A variety of lecture topics are covered at each class meeting. These topics are intended to help students in the preparation and delivery of their speeches. Lecture topics include: 1) types of informative speeches, 2) outlining the speech using the keyword outline approach, 3) patterns of organization, 4) audience analysis, and 5) a summary of nonverbal communication concerns for the public speaker.

At a minimum, lecture and individual speech instructions seek to ensure students: 1) speak loud, clear, and slow; 2) employ effective eye contact with the audience; 3) use keyword outlining; and 4) base their speech content on logical premises. Keyword outlining involves developing an outline using keywords that summarize main points of the speech (rather than writing a complete text of the speech). Having only keywords to speak from helps the student establish eye contact with the audience and avoid reading the speech.

A letter is sent to parents prior to the beginning of the course. Among instructions to parents is a request that parents not plan on waiting for their child in the classroom (to avoid inhibition of students as they speak). The primary function of this letter is to describe intended learning outcomes.

Students receive a course completion certificate at the end of class meeting number three. This certificate acknowledges course sponsorship and completion. It provides a general overview of the course.

I find teaching the course to be an enlightening opportunity. It provides a unique avenue to apply my public speaking instruction skills (outside of the traditional college classroom). Similarly, it provides middle-school students a glimpse of a postsecondary-level educational institution. This can serve as a stepping stone in their precollege goal setting.

Chapter Sixteen

A Systems Approach Analysis of Information Diffusion within an Organizational Telephone Service

In selecting an area of information diffusion for analysis, I placed "usefulness" at the top of my list of criteria. The organization I chose to work with was Delta Tau Delta Fraternity at Ohio University. The area of information diffusion that was examined centers on the procedures used with incoming telephone calls.

As the Proctor (head resident/house manager) of the "Delt" house, it was my intention to select a project that would be beneficial to my own academic needs and the organization that I chose to work with. My initial thoughts on this project were that it might be too minor to effectively analyze. With the project presently completed, I can now see that this was not the case and that the analysis has applications on a larger scale (with other organizations). As for Delta Tau Delta, the project has been useful in improving the diffusion of information received through the telephone.

To operationalize my analysis, I employed a systems approach. This approach consists of five basic steps: 1) Problem Identification/Translation; 2) Analysis (users' needs and responsibilities, internal/external constraints, and criteria for evaluation); 3) Synthesis (identification of possible solutions); 4) Implementation/Operation (of a solution); and 5) Evaluation/Reassessment (of the chosen solution). The systems approach provided a systematic means for examining the problem. Rather than utilizing a "hit-or-miss" approach, it promoted a step-by-step process for working towards an effective solution. This allowed for more concrete decision making (by building on the previous steps of the process).

I. Problem Formulation/Translation

The Delt house houses fifty-two men. Living quarters are divided within four areas of the house: the front hall, back hall, middle hall, and "the pit" (the basement). The house has two payphones (noted in the diagram at the front entrance and the kitchen).

Front Hall

	Middle Hall	
Mail		
Boxes		Back Hall
X Phone		
Front Entrance		
	T.V. Room	X Phone
		Kitchen

"The Pit"

In the past, the procedure for handling incoming calls was for the person answering to either physically locate the person being called or to yell the person's name (hoping that person would respond). If neither procedure produced the person being called, the person answering would "sometimes" leave a message from the caller. It was difficult to estimate the effectiveness/ineffectiveness of this approach, but it has been my contention that a more reliable procedure could be developed. The goal of my research has been to develop a more reliable and consistent procedure for handling incoming telephone calls.

II. Analysis

Assessment of user needs and responsibilities involved basic considerations. The two phones (noted in the diagram) are the only phones in the fraternity house. These phones serve the chapter for a wide range of incoming calls. Such calls include long distance calls from parents, local calls from friends, a variety of messages, etc. The fraternity membership has few responsibilities with regard to the phones. The chapter pays fifty dollars a month to maintain the phones in the house. There are no designated individuals who are responsible for answering the phone or conveying phone messages.

There were considerations, with regard to external and internal constraints, which had to be recognized in laying the groundwork for possible solutions. Externally, there were limited funds available for the implementation and maintenance of possible solutions. Examination of the housing constitution showed that such expenditures could be allocated from the general fund. As is the case with most student organizations, extra money was not abundant. After conferring with the fraternity administration council, I was informed that no set amount could be set aside without knowing what the proposed solution was. Assuming this meant to work towards an economical solution, I agreed to work within those guidelines.

Another external constraint was that there is very limited literature available in this area of research. Looking primarily under headings of "telephone," "information diffusion," "information services," and other related topics produced, for the most part, information that was too technical (dealing more with electrical circuits and transmissions rather than with the aforementioned). At the other extreme was information dealing with phone etiquette that was not specific enough for my needs. My foremost time constraint was that I wanted to complete the project by the middle of June so it could be submitted at the end of spring quarter.

Internal constraints were vague. Primarily, I needed the cooperation of the fraternity members to implement a system. I decided that an important aspect within this consideration would be to find a solution that involved an uncomplicated process.

Another internal constraint dealt with in-house vandalism. I have experienced a variety of housing situations (for fifteen to twenty-five-year-old males) ranging from military barracks, to university housing (Greek and non-Greek), to apartments, to houses, to camping (cabins). It has been my observation that (minor) in-house vandalism is somewhat prevalent with this age group. It should be no surprise that such vandalism will most likely increase in environments that promote the consumption of alcohol and other mind-altering chemicals. Although I do not advocate such practices, these are factors that I have taken into consideration during the analysis stage. In-house vandalism includes any action ranging from using the implemented solution for any reason other than its intended purpose to malicious destruction of the constructed materials.

In formulating criteria for evaluation, the most basic criterion was that the telephone message should get through to the person being called. Ideally, it would be preferable for the person being called to come to the phone but, under the circumstances, it was more realistic to work toward insuring there is a message left for the person being called. Thus, the only thing lost is time. Of course, given emergency situations, the caller could relay the importance of the call to the person answering and thus work towards a more expedient means (i.e., physically locating the person being called).

As previously mentioned, monetary resources would only allow for an economical solution. The solution would need to be economical and dependable for such research to be worthwhile. Within these parameters, any improvement would be welcomed.

III. Synthesis

In working to identify solutions, I consulted the General Telephone Company of Ohio, observed procedures used by other university housing situations, recounted my own group living experiences, and reviewed available literature on the topic.

One article ("Private telephones tie a campus together," 1980) dealt with the problem of telephone information diffusion in an article about Pomona College (Pomona, California). One of the group living experiences I recounted, before finding the article, was my time as an exchange student at Pomona College. During the time (1976) I lived in a dormitory that housed roughly seventy people and we had four payphones in the dorm. Our problems were similar to those described at the Delt house.

Unfortunately the research focused on the campus-wide problem rather than the individual dormitories. The article discusses how the university bought a whole system for their own use. This improved all aspects of campus telephone use.

My contact with the General Telephone Company of Ohio evidenced (ironically) the need for improvement in our telephone information dissemination at the Delt house. When I never heard from the Athens area service manager, I contacted his office and found that he had called the Delt house a month earlier. I didn't get the message.

After consulting, recounting, reviewing, and observing our situation I developed four possible solutions. These included: 1) install a phone in every room; 2) install a P.A. system in each of the four areas of the house; 3) install a phone in every room with a system whereby only incoming calls could be transferred; and 4) the use of mailbox notes for phone messages. In following with the systems approach, these possible solutions were measured against the criteria for evaluation.

Installation of a phone in each room would be dependable as each phone would be servicing only two people. The main drawback is that it would be too costly for our budget.

Through the use of a P.A. system (speakers in each area of the house) the person answering could merely page the person being called. Although this system would be effective if the person being called was in the house, it does little to insure a message would be left if he is gone from the house. The P.A. system would not be expensive as one had been used two years earlier and the wiring and three of the speakers were still in place. The system was discontinued due to in-house vandalism and because it was used for reasons other than telephone calls (pranks, etc.).

Installation of phones in each room, which can only take incoming calls, was too expensive. With this system, the person answering would need to channel the call to the resident's room. This system would do little to insure the noting of messages (should the resident not be home). My experience is that this system might also fall prey to in-house vandalism.

With in-house vandalism receiving such strong consideration, it might seem logical to deal with this aspect as the problem. This was considered initially, but due to the length of the term, it was decided to deal with it as a "given."

The fourth solution centers on the use of mailbox notes. With this system, blank notes are available at both phones. If the caller cannot be located, a message is left for him in his mailbox. The mailboxes are located beside the phone at the front entrance of the house. Roughly 80 percent of our calls go to that phone. This system would not be expensive. Costs would be limited to paper, pencils, and an apparatus for holding the paper at each phone. This approach would also be dependable in getting messages to those who were called, as residents check their mailboxes daily (except Sunday). *A Good Housekeeping* article ("Plan a Telephone Center," 1971) elaborates on this belief in emphasizing the importance of having phone messages posted within the pattern of daily activity. From my experience, I felt this system would not be subject to in-house vandalism as there wasn't much material to vandalize. Also, if the high regard held for mail is shared with phone messages, then the phone messages would not be tampered with.

IV. Implementation/Operation

After evaluating the four solutions against the criteria for evaluation, I decided to implement the mailbox notes system. Initially, I posted a "pronged" clipboard at each phone. Blank message sheets were attached on the prongs so they could be torn off the clipboard easily. On each sheet were the words "name" and "message." I used pink paper so the residents could easily notice they had a phone message (in contrast to the gold mail slots and usual white mail envelopes). A pencil was attached to each clipboard.

Before installing the system, I addressed the residents at their weekly fraternity meeting. These meetings are well attended. I briefly explained that I was trying to improve the "phone problem" in the house. The instructions were simple. "When you answer the phone, yell or contact the person being called. If you can't locate the person, at least leave a note for the person in his mailbox." In closing, I mentioned that they should be sure to check their mailboxes regularly for messages as well as mail. It was my belief that the system would be perceived as an extension of me. It was received without criticism or question.

V. Evaluation/Reassessment

On the fourth day after the system was implemented, the pencils and clipboards were stolen. Considering that each clipboard was only hanging from the wall on a nail, I didn't view this as a major drawback.

After working with the house manager, we installed an apparatus that would require serious destructive intent (and a crowbar) for its removal. The board and prongs were bolted into the wall. It has been used efficiently since then.

The evaluation/reassessment stage has consisted of (brief) survey interviews, an experimental procedure, and observation. The survey interviews were conducted by talking with at least three members of each of the four sections. The open-ended questions dealt with their observations of the effectiveness of the system and any suggested improvements. These were all favorable; there were no suggested improvements.

In "Simple test for telephone courtesy" (Taylor, 1971), an experiment was described whereby two new City Hall employees in Inglewood, California, called an extensive list of City Hall phone numbers to request information. There were two types of questions; a routine question about city trash collection and calls for a nonexistent person (James Wilbur). These questions were asked through separate phone calls. Each person answering was graded by the experimenter with regard to alertness, friendliness, distinctiveness, desire to help, and attitude.

Using a similar approach, I called three residents from each section of the house (when I knew they were gone) over a three-day period. With each call I requested that the person answering take a message for me. (Since there were only twelve calls made, I told each person who received a message that I was merely running a test on the system and that it wouldn't happen again.) After making the calls, I checked the individual mail slots (for those persons I tried to contact) and found that out of twelve calls made there were twelve messages left.

Another approach was to number the slips of paper to get an idea of how many messages were left each day. Over a two-week period, there were roughly fifteen messages a day; weekend messages were more prevalent.

Observation showed that the message slips were used for other types of messages aside from phone messages. Such unintended messages included "please return my tennis racket," "meet us at The Phase," etc. I observed these messages by looking for pink sheets in the mailbox slots. During the two-week period there were a few "illegitimate" messages left in the boxes that were clearly pranks.

My apartment (in the house) was located within hearing distance of the main telephone. This allowed for observation of how the system worked. From my random observations, it is my opinion that the system worked primarily because it takes very little effort for the person answering to write a message and then place it in the appropriate mailbox. One drawback that could occur would be that a person answering the phone might show less effort in finding a resident because he knows a written message will fulfill the obligation.

Overall, I believe a stationary apparatus (for holding the message sheets) will be the base for the system's success. Results, thus far, have shown that cooperation exists if the paper and pencils are there.

Notes

"Plan a Telephone Center," *Good Housekeeping*, 172, March 1971, 188.

"Private Telephones Tie a Campus Together," *American School and University*, 52, March 1980, 72.

Taylor, D. "Simple Test for Telephone Courtesy," *American City*, 86, May 1971, 134.

Chapter Seventeen

Researching Cross-Cultural Relations among Varied Racial/Ethnic Groups via C-SPAN Videotapes

In recent years the academic community has recognized C-SPAN (Cable-Satellite Public Affairs Network) as a valuable teaching tool in the classroom. This chapter will describe how C-SPAN can be used for communications oriented research. Discussion of this undertaking emphasizes methodology, thus enabling the reader to realize possible applications in his or her own research area.

Within my particular research area, cross-cultural issues related to U.S.-China relations, I have focused on reaction in the United States to the Chinese pro-democracy movement using C-SPAN as a representative forum for discussion on the issue. C-SPAN is a representative forum because it does not have a political agenda it is promoting. I will present this project in sequential steps.

1) Primary funding for this research was obtained through a C-SPAN faculty development grant ($500) and an additional $350 was granted by C-SPAN in recognition of my participation at a C-SPAN seminar for professors. Funding can obviously be acquired through a variety of means within the faculty member's institution.

2) I then contacted the Public Affairs Video Archives at Purdue University. Tapes of all C-SPAN programs since 1987 are indexed at the Archives and are available from the organization. I requested from them a selected listing of programs dealing with reforms in China. They prepared and sent me an annotated list of eighty-two programs (ranging in time from thirty minutes to ten hours and ranging in cost from $30-$275).

3) Twenty-one programs were selected based on their relevance to the Chinese pro-democracy movement. Types of programs included forums, news conferences, speeches to the National Press Club, roundtables, speeches, House Committees, call-in shows, House Highlights, Congressional News Conferences, Senate Committees, and book reviews.

4) While viewing the tapes I prepared notes and, based on observed consistencies, decided to interpret the tapes through analysis of the high-context/low-

context messaging. That is, the high-context channels of communication used by Chinese speakers conflicted with low-context channels of communication used by Americans. This exemplifies a standard cross-cultural communication dynamic. Analysis focused on responses by President Bush, U.S. political representatives, Chinese students studying in the United States, Chinese diplomatic representatives, and the American public.

Chinese speakers typically use high-context channels of communication that tend to be less direct and heavily reliant on nonverbal messages. American speakers typically use low-context channels of communication that tend to be more direct and based on literal verbal statements. Cross-cultural misunderstanding can easily occur when interactants are using different channels on the high-context versus low-context continuum.

5) This analysis is appropriate for publication in academic journals (in written form). More unique, however, it is appropriate for video presentation at professional conferences (using excerpts from the C-SPAN programs). This obviously provides illuminating context for the findings. One can argue that use of such tape excerpts are more valuable than traditional footnoting in written formats.

6) These videotape presentations comprised of C-SPAN excerpts and my interpretive narration can then be used as innovative teaching resources. Feedback from colleagues at professional conferences can be useful in sharpening the focus of the presentations. Findings from this analysis can benefit student understanding in a variety of courses in the communication arts curriculum including Mass Media, Persuasion, Cross-Cultural Communication, Rhetorical Communication Theory, Interpersonal Communication, and Public Speaking.

There are many who argue scholarly research is done at the expense of time that can be put towards effective teaching. Use of C-SPAN in the aforementioned manner allows the faculty member to competently meet both objectives.

Those interested in obtaining more information about C-SPAN and the Public Affairs Video Archives may contact the following:

C-SPAN
400 North Capitol Street N.W.
Suite 650
Washington, D.C. 20001
800-523-7586

Public Affairs Video Archives
Purdue University
1025 Stewart Center, G-39
West Lafayette, IN 47907-1025
800-423-9630

Index

About the Author

James A. Schnell is a Professor of Communication Studies at Ohio Dominican University in Columbus, Ohio, where he has achieved Master Teacher status. He completed his Ph.D. at Ohio University in 1982 and has authored six books, more than fifty book chapters and journal articles, and more than 120 conference presentations dealing with a variety of contemporary communication issues. He is a Fulbright Scholar and has visited China fifteen times where he has taught as a visiting professor at Northern Jiaotong University (Beijing, China). Schnell served as Chairperson of the Language and Culture Area of the American Culture Association between 1985-1997 and is listed in the *Who's Who in Media and Communications*. He is a Lieutenant Colonel in the U.S. Air Force (Reserve), where he is an Assistant Air Attaché to China.